WHY HOLINESS?

WHY HOLINESS?

The Transformational Message That Unites Us

CARLA D. SUNBERG
EDITOR

THE FOUNDRY
PUBLISHING

Copyright © 2019 by The Foundry Publishing
The Foundry Publishing
PO Box 419527
Kansas City, MO 64141
thefoundrypublishing.com

ISBN: 978-0-8341-3807-0

Printed in the
United States of America

Cover Design: Mike Williams
Interior Design: Sharon Page

Library of Congress Cataloging-in-Publication Data
A complete catalog record for this book is available from the Library of Congress.

10 9 8 7 6 5 4 3 2 1

CONTENTS

༄

WHY HOLINESS?

CARLA SUNBERG

When's the last time you had a conversation with someone about your faith in Jesus Christ? There are those who may be curious as to why, in this age of authenticity and rationalism, someone would choose to follow Christ. The circle of questioning may even expand, questioning the place of the church in the life of faith. Further reflection may leave one wondering why—in a world teeming with nondenominational Protestantism and a more generic Christianity—there is a segment of Christianity that chooses to emphasize holiness.

Reaching back into history, we find our spiritual and theological father, John Wesley. This man, who helped lead a religious revival in eighteenth-century England, had an optimistic faith in the transformational work of the Holy Spirit to bear witness to salvation in Christ and the promise of living a sanctified life in the already present kingdom of God. The ministry of the early Methodists literally transformed English society and then made its way to the shores of the newly minted United States. There, circuit-riding ministers passionately carried on with Wesley's message of "scriptural holiness" as they pressed into the frontiers of this new nation. Wesley believed that scriptural holiness was the message to which he was called; therefore, he and the Methodist societies kept this as the central focus of their mission as long as he was alive.

Nearly one hundred years later, a young Methodist minister by the name of Phineas F. Bresee was impassioned by the call to preach scriptural holiness. While he began his life in New York, he later traveled west, spending time in Iowa and eventually ending up in southern California. There were others who were sure that the message of holiness was exactly what the world needed, and suddenly camp meetings began to spring up across the country: groups gathering to make sure the message of holiness as preached by John Wesley would not be lost in the rapid expansion of the church across the face of America. Camp meetings and revival meetings that focused on the message of holiness dotted the countryside, with thousands coming to know Christ. Churches were planted as a result, and all were united in the message of holiness. Pastor Bresee was part of a movement that stretched from the east coast to the west, from the upper midwest and deep into the south.

The focus on holiness created tension among some of the Methodists who had now progressed past their founder and no longer found it vital to preach holiness. Pastor Bresee would call it the push and pull of holiness: the sense of being pushed out of his influential positions in the Methodist Church and the pull of the holiness camp meetings and the optimistic message being preached. He eventually felt God draw him to the down-and-out communities of Los Angeles, preaching the message of holiness that he believed would set the people free. He expanded slightly on Wesley's mantra, believing that this new group, identifying with Jesus as Nazarenes, should preach scriptural holiness and minister to the poor. At the center of it all was holiness—the hope and promise of transformation by engaging in the very present kingdom of God.

A couple of years ago I read a book by Simon Sinek called *Start with Why*, which is a secular book that doesn't speak about the church yet is extremely relevant. Every day, organizations spend time and energy on doing their business. Much of the time the emphasis is on the *what* (what it is that they do) and the *how* (how it is that the work gets done). I'm sure the church has provided us with similar experiences as we have attended numerous workshops and seminars that tell us *what* we ought to be doing and *how* we should get it done. This may relate to our personal spiritual lives or to the work of the church at large. I would argue that we have been inundated with the *what* and the *how* and that we may have grown weary along the way.

Simon Sinek suggests that every great organization starts with *why*. Those who know *why* they do what they do find it much easier to develop their *what* and their *how*. For great organizations, the focus is always on the *why*, and most every member of a great organization can tell you their *why*. Wesley and Bresee both knew their *why*: to preach scriptural holiness. Preaching scriptural holiness was at the very core of the Methodist movement and the birth of the Church of the Nazarene. These people passionately understood the *why* of everything they did. Every activity, every ministry, every *what*, and every *how* was completed in light of their *why*, which was holiness.

About a generation ago, I believe we became confused about our *why*. We began arguing about categories and whether we were American Holiness or Wesleyan. Was holiness about purity and following a set of rules, or was it about love? Somehow we thought we had to choose one or the other. In our disagreements, something got lost. Instead of wrestling with our *why* and allowing it to remain our driving force, it became easier to teach about the *what* and the *how*. We established conferences to teach the latest techniques when it came to the attractional church, building a Sunday school, or how to facilitate small groups. We became obsessed with style of worship and whether (and how often) to celebrate the Lord's Supper. Somewhere along the way, we may have forgotten about asking *why*.

I didn't attend seminary until I was nearly forty. By the time I was able to go and sit in classes, I was hungry to learn more about this church of which I had been a part since my birth. Day after day, whether in class or soaking up the reading assignments, I was en-

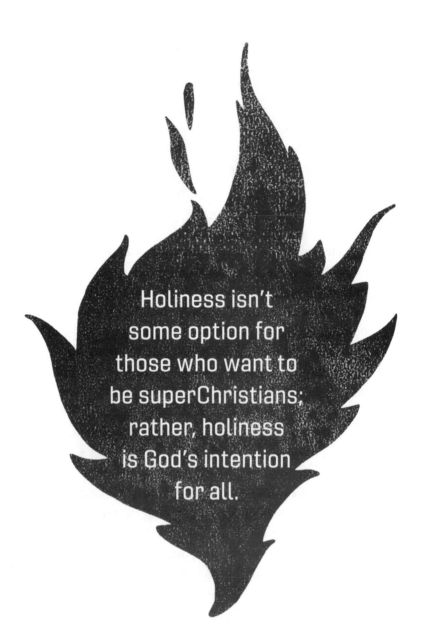

Holiness isn't some option for those who want to be superChristians; rather, holiness is God's intention for all.

lightened about our understanding of holiness. I will never forget studying the Trinity in my systematic theology course and, there, finding a God of love existing in holy fellowship—to which I was invited. It was an overwhelming thought that only continued to build as I discovered that Christ's incarnation created a pathway for humanity to be restored in the image of God. Here was God's idea all along—that all of humanity would be holy, just as God is holy. Then I experienced my "aha" moment: the discovery that holiness isn't some option for those who want to be superChristians; rather, holiness is God's intention for all. Holiness is at the core of everything that is God and is revealed in Christ. Suddenly I wasn't just in the church because I had been born into it. Instead, this was a theology that resonated deep in my heart and soul. Our message of holiness satisfied my own spiritual hunger.

As a holiness church, the Church of the Nazarene and its sister denominations have an incredible birthright that comes with responsibility. We are the heirs of those who were called to preach scriptural holiness, and we are to be stewards of that calling. Everything we do should be defined by our *why*—and that is holiness. The beauty of this message of holiness is that it has the potential of resonating with the needs of our world. Holiness draws us into relationship with our transcendent God, a place of mystery that is beyond our ability as humans to define. This place is where we learn that we can live victoriously, beyond the sin that so easily entangles—because the love of a holy God can set us free. Holiness invites us into daily living where love of God and love of neighbor provide the impetus for all of life. It is an invitation into participation in Christ and active engagement in the kingdom mission. It is a place of *via media*, a place of tension found in the middle that refuses to be drawn to the extremes. Holiness binds us to the mind of Christ, uniting us until we are one in him.

We are truly a Wesleyan-Holiness people who bring together the best of what the church has had to offer. Instead of being afraid of the holiness discussion, it's time for us to again embrace the impassioned call of Wesley and of Bresee to preach scriptural holiness. This is our *why*, and we shouldn't be afraid to rediscover this driving force. Every *what* and *how* of the church should be defined by our *why*, which is holiness.

The Church of the Nazarene has now become a truly global church. Throughout our missional history, the Holiness Movement has always made theological education a priority. Now, as we take time to emphasize our *why*, we have the privilege of inviting new voices into the conversation. In this volume we will hear from theologians from the Philippines, England, Mozambique, Russia, and the United States who will help us start with *why*.

We are ushered into the conversation by Rev. Dr. Dick Eugenio, who is a professor of theology at Asia-Pacific Nazarene Theological Seminary in Manila, Philippines. He helps us wrestle with why we should reflect God by way of understanding of the Trinity and how God's triune nature provides us with a greater understanding of holiness. Eventually Eugenio brings us into a powerful understanding of the refiner's fire, how impurities are finally removed and we are left clearly reflecting our holy God. The mission statement of the Church of the Nazarene is "to make Christlike disciples in the nations." This can only happen when we know our *why* because Christlikeness is the reflection of our holy, incarnate God.

Rev. Jacob Lett—professor of theology at MidAmerica Nazarene University in Olathe, Kansas, and doctoral student at Nazarene Theological College and the University of Manchester in the UK— helps us understand the need for and role of spiritual formation in the life of a believer. We begin to see holiness as the cooperation of humans with divine grace in the formation of holiness. Examining the letters of John Wesley, Lett helps us understand how Wesley instructed and discipled those who were part of his Methodist societies. He wanted them to understand that they could be entirely sanctified through a simple act of faith and that they were to "expect to be made perfect and to expect it now." This cultivation of holiness is to be lived out in the life of the individual who practices spiritu-

We are the heirs
of those who were
called to preach
scriptural holiness,
and we are to be
stewards of that
calling.

al disciplines. We are to fill our minds with Scripture and become so engaged in kingdom activity that we are transformed by the renewing of our minds (Romans 12:2). This understanding of holiness should be foundational to all discipleship.

One of the features of the American Holiness Movement was the camp meeting and, added to that, revival services. While revivals and camp meetings were primarily about providing opportunities for people to come to know Christ, there was also something more. The idea of "revival" is to revive something that already had life. Maybe the American Holiness Movement understood that even those who have been following Christ already need to continually be encouraged to deepen their walk with Christ. One of the misconceptions of holiness has been that there is no need for spiritual growth after entire sanctification—that, somehow, we have to claim perfection in that moment and that any confession of infirmities after that moment might somehow mean we are not sanctified anymore. So why the need for revival? Because we have had an incomplete understanding of perfection. To be perfect is to be God's holy people because that's what we were created to be. That's Jesus's understanding of perfection: for something to fulfill the purpose for which it was created. We are to participate with God on the journey, drawing ever closer to Christ. The reality is that, from time to time, we may all need revival because life can get in the way of our spiritual growth and development.

Rev. Dr. Filimao Chambo—a general superintendent in the Church of the Nazarene and biblical scholar who is originally from Mozambique—reminds us of the need for revival. Here we find the voice of those who are preparing the way for the Lord, a call to return to the "fullness of life found in the covenantal relationship with God." We are to be the voice that proclaims the hope that is found in the holiness of God, and Dr. Chambo issues us a call to revive our hearts to be refocused entirely upon God.

The condition of the heart influences our actions. Rev. Dr. Diane Leclerc—professor of historical theology at Northwest Nazarene

University in Nampa, Idaho—reminds us of the need for *orthokardia*, or a right condition of the heart. A right condition of the heart is vital if we are to have any discussion of a holiness ethic or Christian action. Leclerc reminds us that any activity in the life of the believer or in the church must be filled with the energy of love that flows from a right heart.

As the heart is made right before God, so we fall deeply in love with our Creator God. When that happens, we participate in fellowship with God, and suddenly our hearts begin to break for the things that break God's heart. Ultimately, Rev. Dr. Deirdre Brower Latz—principal and lecturer at Nazarene Theological College in Manchester, England—reminds us that holiness will always result in an outward focus. This reality has practical implications for the ways in which we live our lives. We must treat people with dignity, for that is holy. We respond to people's needs deeply and compassionately because we are in Christ. The result is a community of faith that is always looking outward, for opportunities to minister. This is the holiness message of Phineas Bresee, who reminded us to preach scriptural holiness and minister to the poor. For him, the two were inseparable, for he understood his *why*.

Rev. Danny Quanstrom, pastoring in Hastings, Michigan, helps us consider the reality of our current context. We are now in uncharted territory, a wilderness where life has become uncertain. The *what* and *how* that we learned just last year will no longer provide us with the necessary paradigms. In the wilderness, we must draw upon the holy practices of worship, which lead us into communion with the transcendent God. Somehow, in that place, we find comfort in that which is beyond our understanding. Worship becomes the place of practice where we learn how to love God and others through the love of Christ.

Finally, we are invited into a conversation with the past. Dr. Olga Druzhinina—director of Russian literature for the Church of the Nazarene and professor of theology—encourages us to mine from the past and allow it to influence our current understanding of holiness. As the Church of the Nazarene continues to spread global-ly, we are encountering cultures with a long and rich heritage. There we find that there are intersections, or places of dialogue, with the past that make our understanding of holiness richer and fuller. We know that John Wesley spent time reading the early church fathers and that they informed his understanding of holiness. Today we are blessed by new theologians from within our holiness tradition who are able to draw from their own cultural heritage to bring additional colors to the palette of our theological canvas. Rev. Dr. Druzhinina invites us to see holiness within the context of Russia. She reminds us, however, that when we engage with a different culture, or with the past, we have to guard our holiness message. We can't allow it to be misinterpreted by culture because of potential false assump-tions. At the same time, we have the opportunity to engage with the past and have theologically coherent discussions while not allowing ourselves to be limited by the traditions of the past. Finally, we are reminded of a vitally important truth, and that is that we must all find ways to start with *why*, and we must live a holy life within every culture we may intersect. We have to find appropriate ways to model holiness before the people to whom we may be sent.

So, why holiness? Because we have been entrusted as heirs of this transformational message that, when preached, has ignited the world. We are to be stewards of the beautiful gift that has been handed to a new generation. There are times when we need to talk about the *what* and the *how*, but may we never, ever forget our *why*.

1
WHY REFLECT GOD?
A Trinitarian Theology of Holiness
DICK O. EUGENIO
ᏕᏬ

When I entered Asia-Pacific Nazarene Theological Seminary as a first-year student in 2003, I was asked to stay in the newly assigned men's dormitory on campus. The building had been the women's dormitory the year before, which helped explain why, upon arriving, I found my room filled with posters of flowers, dogs, and other stereotypically feminine decor. I removed all of the existing decorations except one—a small poster of a dog and a cat hugging each other with a caption that read, "We are so different from each other that we have so much to share."

Such a striking caption proved to be true over my next two years at the seminary, as I interacted with my international roommate and other peers and professors who were different from me. The wisdom of the poster, however, became much clearer to me when I was in Manchester, England, immersed in the doctrines of salvation and the Trinity for my doctoral studies. It struck me how the study of the triune being of God is beneficial to Christian practical spirituality and missions. John Wesley was right: "The knowledge of the Three-One God is interwoven with all true Christian faith, with all vital religion."[1] In particular, as a Christian who grew up in the Nazarene Church, I was so thrilled about the relationship between the doctrines of holiness and the Trinity. This excitement was further fueled by my conversations with my doctoral advisor, Dr. Thomas A. Noble. Since then, I have become convinced that a proper *theo*-logy of holiness needs to be grounded in the being of the *Theos*.[2] Our theology of holiness needs to be God-centered. The command "Be holy, for I am holy" (Lev. 11:44-45; 19:2; 20:7; 1 Pet. 1:16, NRSV) spells in bold letters that holiness is not an abstract concept or a legal command; rather, it is the call to imitate and reflect the character of God.

The beauty of understanding holiness in light of the being of the triune God can be especially appreciated in the context of the local church, with all the dynamics of leadership, ministry involvement, and multifaceted relationships. In the body of Christ, the Christian life is not an individualistic journey of Christians who meet on Sundays solely to recharge and receive guidance through the pastor's sermon in order to make progress in their private holiness quests. Holiness is also not exclusively a moral goal comprised of perfect outward performance based on what the pastor preaches for and against. Holiness is communal-relational. The church—as a body with all of her members—is called to be holy just as her Lord is holy. She is God's "holy nation" (1 Pet. 2:9), a community of faith called together from darkness to light in order to participate in God's divine nature (2 Pet. 1:4).

So how does the church as a body appropriate to herself the divine command to "be holy, for I am holy?" The command gives an obvious hint that God himself is holy. Although we can affirm that God's holiness refers to God's character and attributes, perhaps it

---

1. John Wesley, "On the Trinity," in *The Works of John Wesley*, vol. 2, *Sermons II, 37–70*, ed. Albert C. Outler (Nashville: Abingdon Press, 1985), 385.

2. For a more elaborate treatment of this topic, see the excellent work of T. A. Noble, *Holy Trinity: Holy People: The Theology of Christian Perfecting* (Eugene, OR: Cascade Books, 2013).

is even better to say that God's holiness is God's nature or essence. The ensuing question, thus, is: What is the nature of God?

Community of Persons

"In the beginning was the Word [God]," John writes in his Gospel (1:1). Before time and space, God was. Because God is triune, therefore, the communion of Persons—the triune God—represents what eternal reality is. Leonardo Boff rightly asserts that "community is the deepest and most fundamental reality that exists."[3] Since the 1950s, the revival of Trinitarian studies has corrected the mistaken perception of God as an aloof, poker-faced deity, advocated since the Middle Ages' insistence that God was the unmoved mover. Since God is triune, God is primarily a communion rather than a solitude. Borrowing from the Eastern Church, particularly the Cappadocian Fathers, many started to advocate for "social Trinitarianism," asserting the social dimension of God's being.[4] When we think of God, we should think of the Three-in-One and One-in-Three.

The implications of our view of God on our understanding of earthly realities are staggering. For example, we may pause a bit and ask: if we are created in the image of God, who is a communion of Persons, are we not also called to be a communion of persons as human beings? In the movie *I, Robot,* Dr. Alfred Lanning asks a series of questions that can be posed regarding humans as well: "Why is it that, when robots are stored in an empty space, they will group

---

3. Leonardo Boff, *Holy Trinity, Perfect Community,* trans. Phillip Berryman (Maryknoll, NY: Orbis Books, 2000), 4.

4. For those who strongly adhere to this idea, see Cornelius Plantinga Jr.'s "Social Trinity and Tritheism," 21–47, and David Brown's "Trinitarian Personhood and Individuality," 48–78, in Ronald Jay Feenstra, Cornelius Plantinga, eds., *Trinity, Incarnation, and Atonement: Philosophical and Theological Essays* (Notre Dame, IN: University of Notre Dame Press, 1989); see also Cornelius Plantinga Jr., "Gregory of Nyssa and the Social Analogy of the Trinity," in *The Thomist* 50, no. 3 (July 1986): 325–52; and Miroslav Volf, "'The Trinity Is Our Social Program:' The Doctrine of the Trinity and the Shape of Social Engagement," *Modern Theology* 14, no. 3 (July 1998), 405–23.

Humans are drawn
to create or join
communities. There is
a sense of uneasiness
in isolation.

together rather than stand alone? How do we explain this behavior? Random segments of code? Or is it something more?" Humans are drawn to create or join communities. There is a sense of uneasiness in isolation. Our "bumping" with one another is not accidental but is an integral part of our creaturely codes. Holiness cannot be separated from our relational and community-seeking nature as human beings.[5] We are called to be in relationships, vertically with God and horizontally with others.

Sin should be understood as the *corruption* of our relational nature and purpose. As Mildred Bangs Wynkoop writes, sin "is a rupture of fellowship with God."[6] Sin is the *negation* or absence of relationships. It is to be an individual. It is alienation caused by selfishness. Individualism is the direct opposite of being a person because it means "creating distance . . . [which] ultimately leads to death."[7] Humans are not like territorial animals who growl at others trying to enter their spaces. Instead, we are created in the image of the triune Persons who initiate and invite others into relationship. "God created man in his own image," Karl Barth writes, "in correspondence with his own being and essence . . . God is in relationships, and so too is the man created by him. This is his divine likeness."[8] The life of holiness, therefore, means experiencing a change from an individualistic orientation to becoming a loving and embracing person,

---

5. Whether we care to admit it, there is a connection between the renewal of awareness of the doctrine of the Trinity in the 1950s and the relational emphasis on holiness in the succeeding years.

6. Mildred Bangs Wynkoop, *A Theology of Love: The Dynamic of Wesleyanism* (Kansas City, MO: Beacon Hill Press of Kansas City, 1972), 156.

7. Miroslav Volf, *After Our Likeness: The Church as the Image of the Trinity* (Grand Rapids: William B. Eerdmans Publishing Company, 1998), 81. Colin E. Gunton offers a related comment: "Space is the problem: individualism is the view of the human person which holds that there is so much space between people that they can in no sense participate in each other's being." See Gunton, *The Promise of Trinitarian Theology*, 2nd ed. (London: T&T Clark, 1997), 109.

8. Karl Barth, *Church Dogmatics: The Doctrine of Creation*, 3:2 (Edinburgh: T&T Clark, 1960), 324.

regardless of differences. It is to live in such a way that our being is not one of opposition but of communion.

The communion that God is, furthermore, is not inward-looking. We stand in awe of the fact that God created beings other than himself to be welcomed into the already perfect communion. God is not aloof and distant but a fellowshiping God, "free to go outside of himself, and to share in the life of his creatures and enable them to share in his own eternal life and love."[9] It is not enough to say that the Trinity is a community; it is "an open, inviting, uniting, and integrating community"[10] that is open for all. In this light, the parallel between the triune communion and the church is striking. As the community God established on earth, the church mirrors God as a communing and inviting fellowship. The church is called not only to gather but also to reach out to the other. The embracing inclusiveness of God in creating even his opposite (i.e., Creator-creation, Infinite-finite) for the sake of communion is reflected in his command to love the other, even our enemies. This, for Jesus, is what it means to be perfect just as the heavenly Father is perfect (Matt. 5:48). The holiness and mission of the church are inseparable.

Unity in Diversity

The church's calling to embrace the other reflects the unity-in-diversity of the Trinity. The three Persons of God are different from one another. Although they share the same essence, each Person is distinct from the others. For instance, in the work of salvation, only the incarnate Son was crucified and only the Holy Spirit fills humanity. Although they have different roles in salvation, they are united as one in purpose and will. While the Father is not the Son or

---

9. Thomas F. Torrance, *Trinitarian Perspectives: Toward Doctrinal Agreement* (Edinburgh: T&T Clark, 1994), 2.

10. Jürgen Moltmann, "Perichoresis: An Old Magic Word for a New Trinitarian Theology," in M. Douglas Meeks, ed., *Trinity, Community, and Power: Mapping Trajectories in Wesleyan Theology* (Nashville: Abingdon Press, 2000), 117.

the Holy Spirit, the Son is not the Father or the Holy Spirit, and the Holy Spirit is not the Father or the Son, they are one in communion and action.

The many admonitions in the Bible to live in unity and harmony should be considered as the calling of the church to mirror the nature of God. The command to "be holy, for I am holy" can be translated as "be one, for I am One." The close relationship between holiness and unity is spelled out well in Hebrews 12:14: "Make every effort to live in peace with everyone and to be holy; without holiness no one will see the Lord." Holiness in this verse is not an individualistic moral quest; it is living in unity and harmony. Holiness is *shalom*. Holiness in the church means harmonious relationships. In fact, according to Elizabeth Achtemeier, righteousness refers primarily to "the fulfilment of the demands of a relationship, whether that relationship be with [humans] or with God."[11] The holy, therefore, is the one who preserves the peace and wholeness of the community. Likewise, the wicked is the one who destroys the community and its harmony by sowing discordant seeds, gossiping, or just plain trouble-making. This is why blessed, indeed, are the peacemakers (Matt. 5:9) because they mediate conflicts and initiate restoration of broken relationships (see Acts 7:26; Eph. 4:3; James 3:18).

We must take note that we are called to "make every effort" to be united (see Rom. 14:19 and Eph. 4:3). Holiness is the gift of God, but it is also our responsibility. "If it is possible," Paul writes, "as far as it depends on you, live at peace with everyone" (Rom. 12:18). Certainly, maintaining unity in a congregation with diverse cultural, educational, social, and economic demographics is not easy. The reality is that, while diversity is a beautiful blessing, it exposes the body of Christ to challenges. So what do holiness and unity look like in a church with diverse members? In the church, there are people who

---

11. Elizabeth R. Achtemeier, "Righteousness in the OT," in George Arthur Buttrick, ed., *The Interpreter's Dictionary of the Bible: An Illustrated Encyclopedia* (Nashville: Abingdon Press, 1962).

are more educated, more economically well off, or more respected because of their age or achievements. But this reality does not need to be a source of disunity. The Casting Crowns song "City on the Hill" reminds us about what happens when we allow our differences to divide us. The reasons for the tragedy of the church, the song narrates, were that:

> The poets thought the dancers were shallow
> And the soldiers thought the poets were weak
> And the elders saw the young ones as foolish
> And the rich man never heard the poor man speak

When our distinctions cause us to be proud of ourselves and we begin to look down on others, we destroy the one body of Christ. Of course, our holiness goal is not flat equality because this is an unrealistic dream. Ellen K. Wondra asserts that all earthly relationships are inescapably asymmetrical.[12] Our goal is not egalitarianism or communism; it is reciprocity.[13] As the Casting Crowns song affirms, what we need is a culture of reciprocity in which we are all givers to and receivers of each other's distinctiveness. We need each other, and we grow by relying on the diversity of each other's spiritual gifts:

> It is the rhythm of the dancers
> That gives the poets life
> It is the spirit of the poets
> That gives the soldiers strength to fight
> It is fire of the young ones
> It is the wisdom of the old
> It is the story of the poor man
> That's needing to be told

---

12. Ellen K. Wondra, "Participating Persons: Reciprocity and Asymmetry," *Anglican Theological Review* 86, no. 1 (Winter 2004), 57–73.

13. I have dealt with this idea more fully in "The Church at the Table," *Didache* 13, no. 2 (January 2014), 1–10.

When we mutually reciprocate with one another in the church, we not only have harmony, but the church is also "built up until we all reach unity in the faith and in the knowledge of the Son of God and become mature, attaining to the whole measure of the fullness of Christ" (Eph. 4:12b–13). Diversity in the church may be used for our own advantage. When we help each other, we keep the unity of the body, spur one another to growth, and ultimately mirror the triune God. This is holiness.

Self-emptying and Other-glorifying

"The Trinity," for Thomas F. Torrance, "is by nature a communion of love in himself, who creates a community of personal reciprocity in love."[14] This relationship of reciprocity is characterized by a self-emptying mindset and an other-glorifying disposition. We are familiar with the self-emptying of Jesus Christ and his consequent exaltation (Phil. 2:6–11), but we often miss the fact that the other two Persons of the Trinity share the same experience. A macroscopic reading of the Bible reveals that, in the Old Testament, the Father empties himself by creating excitement about the coming of the Son (Isa. 7:14) and by emphasizing the anointing presence of the Holy Spirit (Num. 11:29; Joel 2:28–30); in the Gospels the incarnate Son empties himself and glorifies the Father (John 17:4) and emphasizes the coming of the Holy Spirit who will bring greater things (John 14:12, 16–17; 16:13–15; Acts 1:8); and the Holy Spirit empties himself by glorifying Jesus Christ (John 16:14–15) and highlighting the Father of the children of God (Rom. 8:15). The Persons of the Trinity empty themselves in order to bring glory to each other. They do not fight for supremacy or draw attention to themselves. Rather, in their works, each one hides to make the other two more visible.[15]

---

14. Torrance, *Trinitarian Perspectives*, 3.

15. The icon of the Trinity painted by Andrei Rublev in the fifteenth century perfectly portrays this remarkable Trinitarian relationship.

The church must possess this self-emptying mindset and other-glorifying disposition in order to be holy as God is holy. Paul was very clear to the Philippians: "In your relationships with one another, have the same mindset as Christ Jesus" (2:5), referring to Christ's self-emptying (vv. 6–8). What does this look like in practice? Paul actually elaborates in verses 2 through 4, writing, "Then make my joy complete by being like-minded, having the same love, being one in spirit and of one mind. Do nothing out of selfish ambition or vain conceit. Rather, in humility value others above yourselves, not looking to your own interests but each of you to the interests of the others." These verses are admonitions to mirror God's holy nature in our relationship with one another. Christians in the church are called to imitate the unity and harmony of the triune communion by possessing the same selflessness and other-centeredness of the Persons of the Trinity.

Paul talks about this again in Romans 12. We Nazarene preachers are often misled by the paragraphing of English translations like NKJV, NIV, and ESV. We unconsciously follow their decision to isolate verses 1 and 2 from the rest of the chapter as one distinct thought. We often preach holiness by using these two verses only, which is a big mistake that can lead to broad interpretations of what "renewing of your mind" means. If we read verses 2 and 3 together, the passage reads like this: "Do not conform to the pattern of this world, but be transformed by the renewing of your mind. Then you will be able to test and approve what God's will is—his good, pleasing and perfect will. For by the grace given me I say to every one of you: Do not think of yourself more highly than you ought, but rather think of yourself with sober judgment, in accordance with the faith God has distributed to each of you."

By reading these two verses together, Paul's intention for the church is revealed in greater clarity. To be renewed in mind is not to think highly of ourselves. To be transformed entails a changing of the mind (Greek *metanoia*, which we often translate as "repentance") not only about God but also about sin and salvation. It also

The church must
possess this
self-emptying mindset
and other-glorifying
disposition in order
to be holy
as God is holy.

means a change of mind about ourselves. The renewed human mind has the mindset of Christ (Phil. 2:5), which, as Paul writes in Philippians 2:6–8, is to think and act like Jesus Christ, "who, being in very nature God, did not consider equality with God something to be used to his own advantage; rather, he made himself nothing by taking the very nature of a servant, being made in human likeness. And being found in appearance as a man, he humbled himself by becoming obedient to death—even death on a cross!" Thus, reading Romans 12 actually reminds us of Paul's primary arguments in Philippians 2 that we should have the same humility and self-emptying mindset of Christ if we hope for one holy church. "The pattern of this world" in Romans 12:2 refers specifically to the world's standards of self-fulfillment and self-worth. The world's definition of power and honor should not have a place in the renewed minds of God's kingdom people.

Continuing on and reading the succeeding verses of Romans 12 brings more clarity. Paul's desire is for the members of the church to be holy and united, which can be achieved in two ways. First, Christians need to live self-emptying lives that are graced with humility. Second, we need to learn to live as children who encourage one another (see Acts 4:36). If the first movement is for us to think not too highly of *ourselves*, the second movement is for us to think more highly of *others*. The first movement is insufficient on its own, which is why Paul admonishes us to "honor one another above yourselves" (Rom. 12:10). The way the ESV translates verse 10 is even more forceful: "Outdo one another in showing honor." The only sanctified competition at church is that of outdoing each other in acts of self-emptying and honoring others. Our task is not to destroy one other through gossiping and backstabbing but to build each other up (Eph. 4:29). In the church, the loser is the one who ends up receiving the greatest honor. The first shall be the last and the last shall be the first (Matt. 20:16; Mark 10:31; Luke 13:30). Furthermore, in order to "live in harmony with one another," Paul makes a plea: "Do not be proud, but be willing to associate with people of low position" (Rom. 12:16).

Life in Love

Paul discusses these same concerns for unity, self-emptying, and other-honoring in 1 Corinthians. But here, he adds and highlights another important component: love. The church of Corinth, although already "sanctified in Christ Jesus" (1:2), is riddled with alarming moral and relational problems. Paul confronts these issues and attempts to solve them by emphasizing love. Shockingly, these problems represent the opposite of what he presents in this chapter as marks of holiness in the church. (There are several issues in the Corinthian church, but we will just deal with those related to our present discussion.) According to Paul, the church is torn apart by divisions (1:10–16; 3:1-9), and they are even taking each other to court (6:1–8). There is discrimination among them, particularly in the celebration of the Lord's Supper, when the rich separate themselves from the poor (11:17–22). Some feel superiority and spiritual pride over others because they believe they have received gifts from the Holy Spirit that display wonders (see chapters 12 and 14). They tolerate the sexual relations between son and mother in their midst, and even boast about it (5:1–5).

Because of all of these things, Paul calls them "worldly—mere infants in Christ" (3:1, 3). They divide themselves continuously through their mindset and actions. Instead of using the gifts of the Spirit to lift each other up, some of them are using them as the basis to affirm and exalt themselves as more spiritual than others. This is why Paul highlights that *pneumatikos* ("spiritual") really means having received the Holy Spirit, an experience they all share (12:3, 13). The Corinthians basically model what the church should not be. Instead of living in harmony or unity, they are divided; instead of self-emptying, they shamelessly affirm themselves before others; instead of being other-honoring, they put others down.

So what is Paul's solution to the Corinthian plague? The answer is 1 Corinthians 13, the "love chapter." This chapter is one of the most taken-out-of-context passages in the Bible. It is read at weddings as if it were about romantic love. The truth is that the chapter must be read in the context of church divisions. In the midst of all the difficulties in the church, Paul admonishes them to love. It begins with a series of rebukes directed toward people who practice their spiritual gifts to exalt themselves and without love of others: "If I speak in the tongues of men or of angels, but do not have love, I am only a resounding gong or a clanging cymbal. If I have the gift of prophecy and can fathom all mysteries and all knowledge, and if I have a faith that can move mountains, but do not have love, I am nothing. If I give all I possess to the poor and give over my body to hardship that I may boast, but do not have love, I gain nothing" (13:1–3).

Then the chapter proceeds to highlight how love should be practiced in the context of social relationships. With the divisions and relationship issues in the church in mind, verses 4–7 narrate what love means in the community that God established: "Love is patient, love is kind. It does not envy, it does not boast, it is not proud. It does not dishonor others, it is not self-seeking, it is not easily angered, it keeps no record of wrongs. Love does not delight in evil but rejoices with the truth. It always protects, always trusts, always hopes, always perseveres." These short statements admonish us to practice the unity, self-emptying, and other-honoring that should characterize the church as a community mirroring the communion of the triune God. At the very center of the church's holiness is love—the love of God and the love that is shared by the members of the body. With the same intent and tone found in Romans 12 and 1 Corinthians 13, Paul also pleads to the Colossians: "Therefore, as God's chosen people, holy and dearly loved, clothe yourselves with compassion, kindness, humility, gentleness and patience. Bear with each other and forgive one another if any of you has a grievance against someone. Forgive as the Lord forgave you. And over all these virtues put on love, which binds them all together in perfect unity" (3:12–14).

That the church should be filled with love is proper because God is a communion of love. "God is love," John writes (1 John 4:8). Augustine famously referred to the Persons of the Trinity as Lover, Beloved, and Love. The church, therefore, can be considered "a created counterpart or reflection of the Trinitarian Communion of Love."[16] The earthly community that is the church is the result of the work of God, whose being is love-in-communion. The church is not only God's creation but also the extension of the perfection and fullness of love that God does not confine within his inner communion. God freely and lovingly moves outward toward others so that they may share the very communion of love, which is God's own life and being. If creation is God's loving act of incorporating the other to himself, reconciliation is God's loving act of re-inviting the other back to union with himself. The church is horizontally a communion of love, a fellowship of reconciliation, a community of the redeemed, and the body whose unity is found outside itself.

Conclusions

A popular sermon illustration narrates a woman's journey of discovery. She wanted to know what Malachi 3:2–3 meant: "He will sit as a refiner and purifier of silver." She called a silversmith and made an appointment to watch him work. She observed how the silversmith was careful and meticulous in every procedure, and she sat silently watching most of the time. Finally, unable to restrain herself, she asked the silversmith, "How do you know when the silver is fully refined?"

He smiled at her and answered, "Oh, that's easy—when I see my image in it."

Our calling, both personally and corporately as a church, is to be "transformed into his image with ever-increasing glory" (2 Cor. 3:18). Like silver or gold being refined, such transformation that ultimately reflects God's holiness may be slow and painful. There is so much we must surrender before God's pleasing will can be accomplished in us. But at least we now know our goal. We already have a starting line and a vision of the end. God is the communion of love,

---

16. Thomas F. Torrance, *Reality and Scientific Theology* (Edinburgh: Scottish Academic Press, 1985), 186–87.

with each of the Persons active in self-emptying and other-glorifying. Our purpose is to reflect this in all of our relationships. This is what it means to "participate in the divine nature" (2 Pet. 1:4). This is what it means to be godly, to be like Christ, and to live in the Spirit.

It is true that we are all very different from one another, but perhaps this is part of God's design for us. In the church, everyone is unique. Each member of the body, including the leaders, possesses his or her own idiosyncrasies, preferences, and quirks. By God's calling, we are all gathered to form the one body of Christ. Because of our differences, we are bound to have divergent opinions on almost everything. But amidst this seemingly chaotic crowd that can produce the craziest swirling vortex of entropy is our holy God, whose grace enables us to understand, tolerate, accept, and forgive in order to become a blessing to others. Only through our Spirit-empowered acts of humility and the prioritization of others may the church be characterized by unity and love. We are not random pieces of broken, colored glass; rather, together we are called to form a beautiful mosaic. We are all different colors and shapes, but we complement and augment each other. The church is one of God's self-portraits in the world, and in his own wisdom, he chose to portray his holiness in a kaleidoscope using redeemed humanity as the privileged resource. Our prayer as a church is that we would do justice to God's design for us.

2
WHY SPIRITUAL FORMATION?

A Trinitarian Reflection on the Formation of Holiness in Wesley's Letters

JACOB LETT

൭൦

What is our role in the work of salvation? What are the practices that lead to the formation of a holy life? If sanctification is the work of God alone, why do humans need to participate in the means of grace? Legalists often seek a righteous life with a passionate, structured discipline that relentlessly pursues God. By contrast, in their attempt to reject legalism, antinomians often pursue the spiritual life passively, trusting in God's sovereign power to transform them without their active participation. A third way of pursuing the holy life exists, which empowers Christians to actively participate in God's transformative grace without the incessant pressure and guilt that comes with legalism or the inactiveness of antinomianism.

In the last thirty years of his life, John Wesley wrote hundreds of letters encouraging Christians to pursue sanctification, a life of perfect love. In these letters, he addresses the questions: Why spir-

itual formation? Why the means of grace? Why human participation? Wesley was a practical and pastoral theologian, who was
concerned about how theology works in the lives of real people and
communities.[1] This emphasis is apparent in his letters, where he is
less concerned with the defense and explanation of his doctrine of
sanctification and more concerned with the spiritually formative ex-
ercises and discipline required of Methodist preachers and laypeople
before and after they are filled with perfect love.

In his letters, we discover a third way of understanding the relationship between divine grace and human cooperation in the formation of holiness. After Wesley's letters on this subject are outlined,
we will reflect on why and how humans are to cooperate in God's
grace to cultivate lives of perfect love through a Trinitarian understanding of salvation.

Wesley's Letters on Divine Grace and Human Cooperation

In his letters, Wesley addresses Christian perfection in various
ways: perfected in love,[2] altogether Christian,[3] sanctification,[4] holiness,[5] and whole image.[6] He uses a variety of images to describe sanctification as a work of grace while also urging his followers to pursue
the work of sanctification. We will first look at how Wesley addresses

---

1. Randy L. Maddox, "John Wesley: Practical Theologian?" *Wesleyan Theological Journal* 23, no. 1 (March 1988): 122–47; David B. McEwan, *Wesley as a Pastoral Theologian: Theological Methodology in John Wesley's Doctrine of Christian Perfections* (Milton Keynes, UK: Paternoster, 2009); Thomas A. Noble, "John Wesley as a Theologian: An Introduction," *Evangelical Quarterly* 82, no. 3 (July 2010), 238–57; Albert C. Outler, "John Wesley: Folk-Theologian," *Theology Today* 34, no. 2 (July 1977), 150–60.

2. John Wesley, *The Letters of John Wesley*, ed. John Telford, 8 vols. (London: Epworth, 1931), 7:219.

3. Wesley, *Letters*, 7:78.

4. Wesley, *Letters*, 7:98.

5. Wesley, *Letters*, 5:6.

6. Wesley, *Letters*, 7:302.

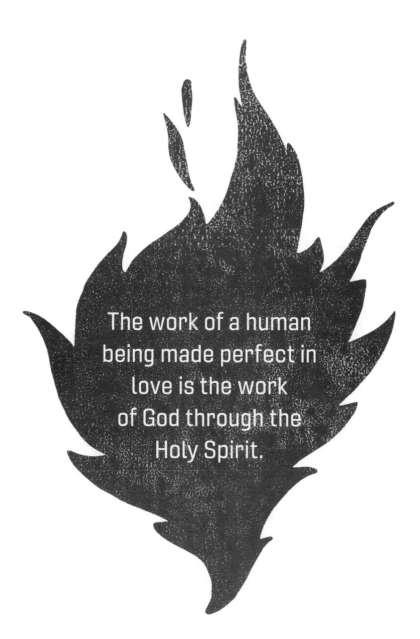

The work of a human
being made perfect in
love is the work
of God through the
Holy Spirit.

the work of God in sanctification, *divine grace*, then focus on the work of humanity in sanctification, *human cooperation*.

Wesley clearly and consistently maintains that the work of a human being made perfect in love is the work of God through the Holy Spirit.[7] He describes the work of God in many ways. God, through the Holy Spirit, leads Christians to perfection.[8] How does God lead? He leads by giving Christians crosses, leading them to prayer, and allowing Satan to tempt them.[9] To an unknown recipient, Wesley describes God's initiative in sanctification: "God is vindicating his right to your whole heart and claiming you for his own."[10] Moreover, he believes it was God who raised up the Methodists to proclaim holiness and lead Christian revivals.[11]

Not only is God the one who leads Christians to perfection, but he is also the Sanctifier who cleanses their hearts and fills them with perfect love. "I know no creature [of the Methodists] who says, 'Part of our salvation belongs to Christ and part to us.' No; we all say, Christ alone saves us from all sin . . . it is all Christ."[12] Wesley is very clear in his correspondence that the Spirit of Christ alone cleanses and sanctifies Christians.[13] Furthermore, he goes on to say that humans are merely partakers of the holiness of God and therefore have no right to claim their sanctification as their own: "For our perfection is not like that of a tree, which flourishes by the sap derived from

---

7. Wesley, *Letters*, 4:10, 39–40, 42, 72, 90, 97, 158, 183, 242–43, 304, 268–69; 5:4, 81–82, 101–103, 112–13, 162–63, 171–73, 186, 202–204, 214–15, 255; 6:29, 37–38, 47–48, 75–76, 82–83, 84–85, 113, 137, 227, 243; 7:76, 78, 80, 156, 162, 227, 246, 263, 277, 293, 302, 322; 8:127.

8. Wesley, *Letters*, 5:173; 6:37, 75, 227; 7:80, 156; 8:127.

9. Wesley, *Letters*, 6:227.

10. Wesley, *Letters*, 7:155–56.

11. Wesley, *Letters*, 5:81, 6:137; 8:238.

12. Wesley, *Letters*, 4:158.

13. Wesley, *Letters*, 4:72, 97, 158, 183, 242–43, 268–69, 304; 5:81, 101–103, 112–13, 171; 6:28, 38, 48, 82–85, 113; 7:76, 162, 226, 246, 263, 266–67, 293, 322.

its own root; but like that of a branch, which united to the vine, bears fruit, but severed from it is 'dried up and withered.'"[14]

Though Wesley certainly maintains that God initiates and completes sanctification in Christians, he unquestionably provides more detailed, significant instruction on the human role in sanctification. Five interdependent themes represent why and how he encourages his followers to pursue sanctification: thirsting and hungering after perfection, simple faith, means of grace, using and increasing grace, and a community that supports and urges perfection.

In approximately thirty-seven letters wherein Wesley gives spiritual advice on seeking perfection, he exhorts his readers to "hunger and thirst," to "groan," and to daily "press" and "labour" after perfection.[15] To Wesley's soteriology, God's work of salvation is enabled in Christians to the degree for which they thirst for perfection. He states, "Indeed if [Christians] are not thirsting after this, it is scarce possible to keep what they have; they can hardly retain any power of faith if they are not panting after holiness."[16] Furthermore, in roughly twenty letters, Wesley insists that believers are not to be content or to rest until they are "altogether Christian."[17] Believers are encouraged to "let your eye be single; aim still at one thing—holy, loving faith, giving God the whole heart."[18] Those who do not experience loving God and neighbor perfectly "may experience it: you surely will, if you follow hard after it."[19] Wesley is clear that God does not typically fill with perfect love those who are not vigorously seeking after it.

---

14. Wesley, *Letters*, 5:202–204. Also see 7:293.

15. Wesley, *Letters*, 4:71, 183, 188, 209, 213, 214, 243, 261, 303; 5:6, 40, 44, 52, 60, 65, 83–85, 94, 171–73, 201, 216, 229–30, 290, 325; 6:29, 37–38, 68, 82–83, 84–85, 113, 153; 7:52, 76, 193, 276, 283; 8:80, 134.

16. Wesley, *Letters*, 5:6.

17. Wesley, *Letters*, 4:51–52, 102–103, 242–43, 260–61, 302–304; 5:51–53, 137, 162–63, 201–202, 229–30; 6:13, 84–85, 274–75, 319; 7:38–39, 98, 132, 191–92; 7:127, 158.

18. Wesley, *Letters*, 6:113.

19. Wesley, *Letters*, 6:213–14.

The nature of thirsting and panting is to "stand fast by simple faith."[20] In his letters, Wesley repeatedly instructs his listeners to receive entire sanctification by a simple act of faith, which occurs in an instant.[21] Christians are to expect to be made perfect and to expect it now.[22] This conviction is evident in Wesley's word to a preacher: "If you press all the believers to go on to perfection and to expect deliverance from sin every moment, they will grow in grace. But if they lose that expectation they will grow flat and cold."[23]

On the other hand, in a letter to Thomas Maxfield, Wesley is quick to point out that faith and expectation cannot be divorced from the means:

> I dislike your saying that one saved from sin needs nothing more than looking to Jesus; needs not to hear or think of anything else; believe, believe is enough; that he needs no self-examination, no times of private prayer; needs not mind little or outward things; . . . expecting the means without the ends; . . . I dislike something that has the appearance of antinomianism, not magnifying the law and making it honourable; not enough valuing tenderness of conscience and exact watchfulness in order thereto; using faith rather as contradistinguished from holiness than as productive of it.[24]

What, then, exactly is this faith that is productive of holiness? Wesley teaches in his letters that the faith productive of holiness is that faith which "worketh by love."[25] To Wesley, sanctifying faith is formed and made perfect through the means of grace.[26] He encourages his believ-

---

20. Wesley, *Letters,* 4:183.

21. Wesley, *Letters,* 4:183, 187, 189, 192–193, 261, 269; 5:16, 39, 84, 112–113, 171–173, 193–196, 210, 214–215, 229–230, 305; 6:238; 7:96, 98, 102–103, 109, 178, 216, 222, 267–68, 283, 293, 295, 317, 322; 8:134, 190.

22. Wesley, *Letters,* 4:188, 242–43; 5:214–15, 229, 290; 6:66, 238, 243; 7:178, 267, 322.

23. Wesley, *Letters,* 6:66.

24. Wesley, *Letters,* 4:192–93.

25. Wesley, *Letters,* 4:175.

26. Wesley, *Letters,* 6:127

ers to act out their faith through sacraments, good works, prayer, and the denying of oneself and the taking up of the cross.[27]

Though Wesley wants to maintain that good works are not required for entire sanctification because God can sanctify a Christian instantly after justification by simple faith,[28] he primarily emphasizes that it is normative for Christians to wait by doing good works.[29] Wesley strongly warns against "quietism," insisting that Christians are not supposed to wait on God to perfect them by waiting in stillness or inactivity but by being zealous for good works.[30] "You cannot keep [sanctification] unless you are zealous of good works. Be fruitful, therefore, in every good work, and God shall see very soon his whole image."[31] Noting the interplay between faith and works, Wesley says, "This is the secret of heart religion—at the present moment to work and to believe."[32]

Another means Wesley often mentions is prayer.[33] Wesley holds that Christians cannot move toward sanctification or retain sanctification without prayer.[34] Wesley challenges a preacher: "Exhort all brethren steadily to wait upon God in the appointed means of prayer and fasting . . . It is a true remark of Kempis, 'The more thou deniest thyself, the more thou wilt grow in grace.'"[35]

The other most frequent means Wesley mentions is that of denying self and taking up one's cross.[36] According to Wesley, God allows Christians to suffer and be tempted, which is part of the per-

---

27. Wesley, *Letters,* 4:303.

28. Wesley, *Letters,* 4:268–269; 7:98.

29. Wesley, *Letters,* 4:172–80, 303; 5:112–13; 6:28, 48, 115, 127, 153, 326; 7:283, 302, 330–31.

30. Wesley, *Letters,* 6:115; 7:26.

31. Wesley, *Letters,* 7:302.

32. Wesley, *Letters,* 5:65.

33. Wesley, *Letters,* 4:97, 103, 243; 5:78, 112–13, 171, 290, 325; 6:48; 7:162; 8:184, 243.

34. Wesley, *Letters,* 5:78; 8:184.

35. Wesley, *Letters,* 8:243.

36. Wesley, *Letters,* 4:43, 103; 5:171, 173, 193–194, 232–233; 6:153; 8:243.

fecting process.[37] Wesley writes, "It is by doing and suffering the whole will of the Lord that we grow up in him that is our head."[38] God allows Christians to suffer, which keeps our inward religion from degenerating and increases our holiness.[39] To sum it up, "There are two general ways wherein it pleases God to lead his children to perfection—doing and suffering."[40]

The fourth theme that is common in Wesley's letters on perfection is that Christians are to seek perfection by using all the grace they have received. By using their grace-empowered faculties, they can then expect to receive more grace.[41] In one of his letters, Wesley warns Miss March of the dangers of being idle, writing, "Nothing would be more likely to hurt the soul than undervaluing the grace already received."[42] The Christian life is always moving forward or backward, and though perfection is instantaneous, gradual growth both precedes and follows it.[43] To John Trembath, Wesley warns, "You cannot stand still; you know this is impossible. You must go forward or backward. Either you must recover that power and be a Christian altogether, or in a while you will have neither power nor form, inside nor outside . . . Do justice to your own soul; give it time and means to grow. Do not starve yourself any longer. Take up your cross, and be a Christian altogether."[44] Wesley often says that Chris-

---

37. Wesley, *Letters,* 5:232–33, 280; 6:48, 75, 82–83, 103; 7:80, 146, 156–57, 194–95, 253.

38. Wesley, *Letters,* 7:80.

39. Wesley, *Letters,* 6:227; 7:253.

40. Wesley, *Letters,* 6:75.

41. Wesley, *Letters,* 4:73; 5: 65, 81, 112–13, 171, 198, 290; 6:38, 66, 82–83, 226; 7:80, 217; 8:184, 243.

42. Wesley, *Letters,* 5:81–82.

43. Wesley, *Letters,* 4:87–88, 103, 163, 187; 5:39, 65, 189, 198; 6:38, 65, 66; 7:80, 96, 102–03, 109, 222, 267, 276, 293; 8:127, 184, 243.

44. Wesley, *Letters,* 4:102–103.

tians are responsible for retaining their perfection as well as maintaining and cultivating growth in perfection.[45]

The final theme that regularly appears in Wesley's letters is the importance of a community that encourages and theologically supports perfection. In numerous letters, Wesley urges his preachers to encourage and exhort others to "go on" to perfection.[46] To one preacher Wesley relates the work of God to the efforts of the preacher: "The more strongly and vigilantly you press all believers to aspire after full sanctification as attainable now by simple faith the more the whole work of God will prosper."[47] To Wesley, the work of God is increased in communities that preach and teach holiness. Along this same line, Wesley also thinks that the work of God prospers when one's theology is sound. This belief can be seen in the number of letters in which Wesley encourages someone to go on to perfection by reading one of his sermons or books.[48] To Mrs. Bennis, Wesley says, "You are frequently sick of a bad disease—evil reasoning; which hinders both your holiness and happiness."[49] Furthermore, Wesley often notes in his letters that antinomian and Calvinist preaching are the greatest hindrance to the work of God in England.[50] In summa-

---

45. Wesley, *Letters*, 4:103, 109, 183, 214; 5:6, 71, 78, 186, 189, 215, 232–33, 265, 90; 6:37–38, 381; 7:194, 246, 273, 293, 302; 8:184, 249.

46. Wesley, *Letters*, 4:235–38; 5:6, 29, 52–53, 77, 83, 93, 209, 290, 344; 6:37–38, 65, 66, 238, 240, 326, 329; 7:102–103, 107, 109, 147, 170, 178, 193, 218, 267, 276, 283, 317; 8:175, 184, 243, 258. Kenneth J. Collins also notices this theme in Wesley's letters, saying, "It was also during the decade of the 1760s that Wesley had become firmly convinced that the Methodist revival would not prosper unless his preachers proclaimed the importance of 'going on to perfection.'" See Collins, *A Real Christian: The Life of John Wesley* (Nashville: Abingdon Press, 1999), 113.

47. Wesley, *Letters*, 7:276.

48. Wesley, *Letters*, 4:243; 5:52, 290, 325; 6:28, 129–30, 137, 153, 326–27, 353, 354; 7:78, 98, 120.

49. Wesley, *Letters*, 5:193–94.

50. Wesley, *Letters*, 4:172–73, 192–93, 208; 5:83–84, 264–65, 344; 6:113, 326.

ry, God's work is hindered in places where perfection is not insisted upon and where holiness teaching and theology are not prominent.

A Trinitarian Reflection on the Formation of Holiness

Wesley is clear that the work of salvation—the formation of holy lives—is the work of God alone (Eph. 2:8–9). At the same time, he undoubtedly stresses that humans must participate in God's work of salvation. When reading his letters, one feels a sense of urgency to pursue holiness. How do we reconcile this? If it is God who ultimately forms holiness, why do we need to cooperate?

I'd like to suggest that we understand divine grace and human cooperation in the formation of holiness through a Trinitarian understanding of salvation, as reflected in Paul's closing words to the church in Corinth: "The grace of the Lord Jesus Christ and the love of God and the fellowship of the Holy Spirit be with you all" (2 Cor. 13:14, ESV). If we let the rhythm of this verse shape our understanding of holiness, and we see that the foundation and possibility of Christian holiness is the "grace of the Lord Jesus Christ," the result is that we are filled with the "love of God," and the means is the "fellowship of the Holy Spirit." In other words, we are sanctified by Christ alone, by grace alone, affirming the Protestant principles of *solus Christus* and *sola gratia*. The movement of grace is the fellowship of the Holy Spirit in God's people. As described by the church fathers, the love of God is cultivated in humanity, the body of Christ, "by the Son in the Spirit."[51] In the context of the incorporating fellowship of the Spirit, the *why* of human cooperation in holiness formation is solidified.

Although the Spirit cultivates holy love in God's people, the Spirit's work is an empowering presence that enables Christians to work out their salvation through the means of grace.[52] Grace is not simply

---

51. Thomas G. Weinandy, *The Father's Spirit of Sonship: Reconceiving the Trinity* (Edinburgh: T&T Clark, 1995).

52. Wesley, *Letters*, 4:158; 6:28; 7:78, 156; 8:127.

Although
the Spirit cultivates holy
love in God's people,
the Spirit's work is an
empowering presence
that enables Christians to
work out their salvation
through the means
of grace.

a divine attitude, wherein God ignores or forgives human sin. Grace is a divine activity and power, through which God restores humanity's ability to love and serve him in the Holy Spirit. Thus, Wesley scholar Randy Maddox calls grace "responsible" or "co-operant" grace, indicating that "Wesley was convinced that, while we cannot attain holiness apart from God's grace, God will not effect holiness apart from our responsive participation."[53] Grace gives humanity the ability to respond and participate. In other words, although humanity's holiness is ultimately a work of the Spirit, the Spirit invites us to cooperate in this work. The Spirit's fellowship of grace is participatory and, as such, is the possibility and the fruit of our cooperation.

Accordingly, Wesley's primary pastoral concern reflected in his letters is that Christians are not making use of their grace-empowered freedom. Normally, the Spirit does not cultivate love in those who wait in inactivity. Wesley was deeply concerned about the antinomian tendencies of the church, which led to laziness and sloth. In one letter, he states, "I find more profit in sermons on either good temper or good works than in what are vulgarly called gospel sermons. That term is now become a mere *can't* word."[54] Many individuals' understanding of the gospel of grace encourages them to do nothing, since it is ultimately God who does everything, whereas for Wesley, grace is the power of Christ's presence in our lives. We are not merely forgiven by grace—we are empowered to participate in works of love.

A helpful metaphor for imagining human cooperation in the formation of holiness is the work of a vegetable gardener. Before it's even warm outside, a gardener is intentionally planning. She plants the seeds indoors. Once they sprout, she blows a fan on the stems to strengthen them. When the weather conditions allow, she tills the garden and transplants, waters, and fertilizes the seedlings. Weeds often attempt to crowd out the young plants, so she fervently works

---

53. Randy L. Maddox, *Responsible Grace: John Wesley's Practical Theology* (Nashville: Abingdon Press, 1994), 19, 147–53.

54. Wesley, *Letters*, 6:326.

toward removing them daily. The gardener's active involvement in the cultivation of vegetable plants continues on and on until harvest and even after harvest. The disheartening part of gardening is that, no matter how hard the gardener works, she can't force the seeds to sprout, the seedlings to grow, or the plants to bear fruit. She can only create the best possible conditions for growth and fruition.

Human cooperation in the formation of holiness is somewhat like this: God, in the Spirit, cultivates love in his people, producing continual growth. Our role in the work of the Spirit is to create the best possible conditions for the Spirit to work. We do this by intentionally participating in the means of grace and in works of love. The means of grace are those practices whereby the Spirit transforms us into the image of love. By participating in inwardly-focused means— the sacraments, personal and corporate prayer, and the proclamation of the Word—the Spirit nurtures our spirits, renewing and restoring love in the people of God. Of course, Wesley also recommends that Christians participate in accountability groups, where we can "watch over one another in love."[55] The Spirit regularly uses other people to come alongside us to make us further into the image of perfect love. The further the people of God inspire one another to pursue the perfection of love, the greater the conditions are for God to do so.

At the same time, God's love throughout Scripture occurs in concrete action for others, through the liberation of his people from the Egyptians, the healing of the sick, God's self-giving love enacted in his death on the cross, and so on. Therefore, Christians should not sit around waiting for God to command them to do works of love but should be quick to participate in those outward means ordained by Scripture. We should seek to liberate the oppressed (Isa. 1:17), provide food and shelter to those in need (Matt. 25:31–46), extend

---

55. John Wesley, *The Works of John Wesley*, vol. 9, *The Methodist Societies: History, Nature, and Design*, ed. Rupert E. Davies (Nashville: Abingdon Press, 1989), 69.

hospitality to foreigners (Lev. 19:34), and take care of the orphan and the widow (James 1:27). As we act out the kingdom of God, the conditions are ripe for the Spirit to shape us into a people of love. The more we intentionally participate in kingdom of God activities, the more God's kingdom will come to fruition on earth as it is in heaven.

When one is renovating their home, it is common to watch HGTV to generate creativity. Popular house-flipping shows form and shape our imaginations, creating design possibilities that would not have existed otherwise. In fact, it may not take long after watching HGTV before one is unhappy with their own home and obsessed with knocking down a wall, installing new countertops, or creating a more open layout. Similarly, the cultivation of holiness occurs when we fill our minds with the images of Scripture and participate in the activities toward which the kingdom of God is oriented. As we do so, our hearts, imaginations, and activities are further formed and shaped by the pattern of Christ (Rom. 12:2).

In conclusion, what we have from Wesley is not a middle way between legalism and antinomianism but a third way. God initiates, sustains, and completes the work of holiness. Yet God invites us to cooperate in this activity. The more we maintain and nurture the work of God, the further grace is increased and the image of love perfected. Divine sovereignty can be overemphasized if it enables human complacency over cooperation and response. Likewise, if the driving force behind human cooperation is the guilt of legalism, it also misses the mark. The foundation of holiness is Christ, resulting in the cultivation of love in his body, the church. This process is the result of the indwelling fellowship of the Holy Spirit. The Spirit normally does not form holiness in those who are not actively seeking after it through the means of grace. Of course, God can do what he wants when he wants, but generally, it pleases God to work in those who would participate with him in the formation of love.

3
WHY REVIVAL?
Make Ready a People Prepared for the Lord
FILIMAO CHAMBO

ͼͽ

"He will bring back many of the people of Israel to the Lord their God. And he will go on before the Lord, in the spirit and power of Elijah, to turn the hearts of the parents to their children and the disobedient to the wisdom of the righteous—to make ready a people prepared for the Lord" (Luke 1:16–17). Like John the Baptist, we are called to make ready a people prepared for the Lord. But how does one do this, and what does it mean to be a people prepared for the Lord?

Throughout the Bible, we find that God calls men and women of different backgrounds to represent him and speak on his behalf to call his people to return to him. In a variety of ways, these men and women go out to the people to make them prepared for the Lord. The call to prepare people for the coming of the Lord is a call to revival. Revival is a call to "re-living," or coming back to the fullness of life found in the covenantal relationship with God. This is a call to a right relationship with God—holy living, unpolluted by sin.

A people prepared for the Lord embrace the call to love God and others in ways that derive only from God's holiness: they are people ready and open to God's love becoming truly complete in them, a people who live as Jesus did (1 John 2:1–11). Luke echoes this by noting, "Many have undertaken to draw up an account of the things that have been fulfilled" through Jesus Christ (1:1). These were things that had been announced by the believers who waited with great anticipation for the day when God would restore his people, resulting in the dawning of new life for them. Luke emphasizes that having a new life in Christ implies that his followers are called to give up their old ways of living. Those who are in Christ should not continue to live in ways that are shaped by the patterns of the world of which they are a part. Of particular interest in Luke is the fact that the worldview of the first-century Christians was shaped mostly by the praxis of the Roman Empire—a world of which they were a part.

Luke proclaims that this new way of life will radically transform the community of people called Israel and the whole creation. Furthermore, the new life in Christ marks the fulfillment of God's promises in the Old Testament. The Lord Jesus Christ comes to incarnate God's way of life for his people. The very same life that the commandments, the law, and the wisdom of the Old Testament expressed as a way of life for the people of God is now revealed in Christ, the Son of God (God-Man). Now, those who return to God, through Christ, will be made a new creation: their sins will be forgiven. In Christ, they can find salvation from sin and from the power of sin. They can live victorious, holy lives while in this world—because Christ makes it possible! This life is possible through Christ, who makes us holy and invites us to remain in him in obedience, wholly devoted to God, and being made holy. In Christ, we are continually made holy! In Christ, humanity can once again experience the fullness of life as the people created in the image and likeness of God.

When God created human beings, he created them in his image and likeness (Gen. 1:27). Adam and Eve were in a covenant relationship with God and remained holy as long as they were wholly God's. But because of sin, humanity became enslaved, unable to untangle themselves from sin and its power—unless they would return to God

God calls his
people to live a
countercultural life
that derives from the
covenant relationship
with him to effect
change in the
world.

for salvation through the forgiveness of sins. But thanks be to God, he did not and will never give up on his creation! God continues to pursue humanity and invites us to live holy lives, as he has designed us. In Genesis 3:15, we already hear God's commitment that he will redeem creation and that sin will not rule forever.

Sin infected God's good creation with evil. Instead of being wholly God's, humanity continues to seek its own sovereignty, and this turns out to be a disaster—a total failure to love others as God intends and to care for the whole of God's creation in ways that reflect God's holiness. Because of sin, humanity's inclination is polluted. This form of life, which ironically may seem to offer a possibility of fantastic future, is instead self-destructive, resulting in pain, suffering, and death. It is no surprise that God does not want his creation to self-destruct because he is full of love and wants everyone to experience the joy and peace found in the fullness of his love. So, even though his people often choose to walk away from relationship with God, God always remains committed to his plan to bring humanity into a right relationship with him. God is committed to restoring humanity and the whole creation. As we read in Genesis 12 and many other passages in the Bible, God brings salvation in partnership with humanity. God's plan is the formation of his holy people, who will partner with him in his holy, redemptive work in the world. Thus, the people of God, who now live their lives following God's holiness, are also called to reflect his holiness in the world.

Notice God's call to Abram: "'Go from your country, your people and your father's household to the land I will show you. I will make you into a great nation, and I will bless you; I will make your name great, and you will be a blessing. I will bless those who bless you, and whoever curses you I will curse; and all peoples on earth will be blessed through you'" (Gen. 12:1–3). God promises to bless Abram and to commission him to be a channel of God's blessing to all peoples on earth. This requires that Abram walk before the Lord and be blameless (Gen. 17:1). This is not a command only for Abram but for all chosen people of God.

Unfortunately, as we know, the descendants of Abraham—in this case, the people of Israel—are often characterized in the Bible as people who, often because of their own doing in disobedience to the Lord, suffer under the rulership of other kingdoms. On the other hand, it is important to note that there are times when the people of God suffer not because of their own doing but because they (we) live in a fallen world characterized by systems that rival God's plan for his creation. In the midst of these systems, God calls his people to live a countercultural life that derives from the covenant relationship with him to effect change in the world. We can conclude that one of the reasons people walk in ways that do not honor God is that they fail to recognize that they cannot make themselves holy. It is God who makes his people holy. So instead of living countercultural lives, the people of God try to live in both worlds. In some ways, they adopt the praxis (way of life) of the world, which is self-destructive.

In adopting the praxis of the world and attempting to live in both worlds—the way of the Lord and the way of the world—the people of Israel become syncretistic idolaters. They include the worship of other gods in their worship of YHWH. Their vision of the coming kingdom of God becomes blurry, as does their vision of what is godly and ungodly. They wander away from their covenant with the Lord. Again, it is important to mention that their praxis upsets God, and at times they face severe consequences for their sins. We also find that God's actions are always redemptive in nature, even when this redemption includes exile or suffering. Through his prophets, God continues to declare that he will bring salvation to his creation in partnership with humanity.

So, for many years, the people of Israel wait with great anticipation for the coming of the kingdom of God—a time when they believe God will rescue them entirely from their woes. They wait for the day when the Lord will restore their prominence as the people of God with the fullness of the benefits promised to their ancestors—a day when all people will know that there is no god like YHWH! It is interesting that, regardless of the state in which Israel finds herself (faithful or unfaithful to the Lord, exile or post-exile, under good or bad kingship), their vision for the coming of the kingdom of God (even when their vision of the kingdom of God becomes blurry) and the possibility of a new way of life with YHWH remains something that they await with great anticipation.

It is significant here to mention that the deliverance of the people of Israel from Egypt serves as a witness that indeed God has the power and authority to redeem his people and that nothing has the power and authority to stop him (see Exod. 15). But beyond God's power and authority to deliver, he also desires to enter into a relationship with his people in ways that will form them into a holy people who are deployed in the world to be a blessing to others. So the Lord gives the law (Exod. 20), which reveals his nature and character to his followers. According to Dennis F. Kinlaw and John N. Oswalt, these laws "are the heart of the covenant that God and Israel [make] with each other. In this sense, they are Israel's vows in her marriage contract with God."[1]

The exodus experience helps the people of Israel shape an optimistic narrative about the coming of the kingdom of God. And, through the voices of the prophets, the vision for full salvation lives on! The Old Testament prophets proclaim that the reign of God will come, and when he comes, his people will be realigned to his holiness and righteousness. Many prophets in Israel work faithfully to make a people ready for the coming of the Lord. In essence, the prophets consistently call the people of God to return to a right relationship with God, which results in also having a right relationship with others (love for God and our neighbors). This more in-depth relationship with God and reflecting of God's love in the world is made possible through the work of God to enable the disobedient and unrighteous people to become the obedient, righteous people of the covenant. And the good news found in the Gospels is the re-

---

1. Dennis F. Kinlaw and John N. Oswalt, *Lectures in Old Testament Theology: Yahweh is God Alone* (Wilmore, KY: Francis Asbury Press, 2010).

minder that the fulfillment of what God was doing through the formation of the Israelites as YHWH's people is now being realized in all of humanity through the coming of Jesus Christ. This happens in fulfillment of what the Old Testament prophets proclaim: "A day will come when all things will be made new . . . a day when a new power will further enable true obedience. There will be a day when God's holiness will be revealed through the radiance of the Son of Man and when he will also say, be holy as God is holy."[2]

The prophets are shaped by the imagination that one needs to remain in intimate relationship with God, for it is through God that one's holiness is derived. They also understand that if they are to represent God and his holiness, they need to hear directly from God, and for this to happen, they need to keep themselves pure so their vision is not blurred by the vision of this world. They believe that this is what God wants for his people, so they seek to declare the Word of God in order to challenge humanity to turn from their evil ways. Their proclamation is "a moral word that comes from a holy God, and its purpose is to turn us from our sins and from our evil. Of course, there is a prediction in the true prophets, but the purpose of that prediction is something very different from divination. Divination seeks to let you know what the future is so you can escape it. The purpose of true prophecy is to let you know who God is so you can get right with him, and in that way, guarantee your future."[3]

Malachi is the last prophet we read about in the Old Testament. He calls the people to repent of their spiritual lethargy. At this time, the people of God doubt God's love (1:2) and justice (2:17) and are lacking in obedience to God and his law. Malachi challenges both the religious leaders and the people of Israel to follow God's ways and worship him as the only Lord. Malachi also announces that God will send his messenger to announce the coming of the Lord (3:1).

---

2. Diane Leclerc, *Discovering Christian Holiness: The Heart of Wesleyan-Holiness Theology* (Kansas City, MO: Beacon Hill Press of Kansas City, 2010).

3. Kinlaw and Oswalt, *Lectures*, 310.

Thus, the work of John the Baptist and his passionate call for the people to repent is viewed as the fulfillment of this announcement.

John the Baptist's ministry begins with the preaching of repentance for the forgiveness of sins. He says, "Repent, for the kingdom of heaven has come near" (Matt. 3:2), calling his audience to turn back to the Lord. According to John the Baptist, it is possible to be in a right relationship with God when Christ forgives our sins. His salvific work is more powerful than sin! In Luke 3:15–18:

> The people were waiting expectantly and were all wondering in their hearts if John might possibly be the Messiah. John answered them all, "I baptize you with water. But one who is more powerful than I will come, the straps of whose sandals I am not worthy to untie. He will baptize you with the Holy Spirit and fire. His winnowing fork is in his hand to clear his threshing floor and to gather the wheat into his barn, but he will burn up the chaff with unquenchable fire." And with many other words,

John exhorted the people and proclaimed the good news to them. Of significance is that John the Baptist is to go in the spirit and power of Elijah. That is, he is to go with the same attitude and spirit, led by the same power that was with Elijah (see 1 Kings 18). Elijah's ministry included being bold to oppose false doctrines. He opposed the worship of Baal; he opposed sin, injustice, and idolatry.

Making ready a people prepared for the Lord includes being bold to confront sin and evil, even when this may be uncomfortable and unpopular. We learn from the prophets, the founding leaders of our denomination, and Wesleyan heritage that they are captivated by the hope of new life that is a possibility for all people who turn to Christ for salvation. They embrace the hope to see humanity and the world transformed through the revelation of God's salvation, and they believe that everyone needs to have the opportunity to hear the good news and to be part of a community that is being formed and matured in God's likeness. This results in a movement of a people of God who are radically transformed and sent into the world to live countercultural lives.

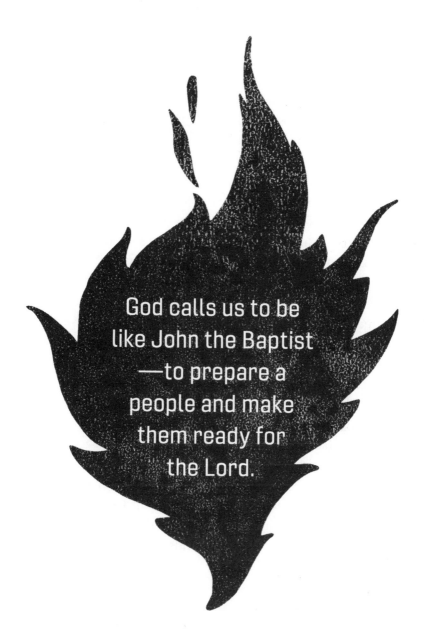

God calls us to be like John the Baptist —to prepare a people and make them ready for the Lord.

This optimism led many—like John Wesley, Phineas Bresee, and others—to proclaim the good news of salvation from sin and the power of sin. They were sold out to the idea that God wants to form his people and then, through and with his people, transform the world. They also understood that such work could only be accomplished in the power of God. They understood the importance of remaining in God as he makes us holy and deploys us to be part of his holy work. Through the power of the Holy Spirit we are able to remain wholly God's.

The Church of the Nazarene was born in a holiness revival. We were born in a movement that was persuaded that God's kingdom is here to do something new, a movement that believed that the kingdom has yet to be revealed to many people in the world (those who have not yet heard), a movement convinced that the one who has come is coming back again and that we must be found in him when he comes again. This is what makes us a people who have always been willing to discern how God wants us to prepare his people for what he is about to do so that all people may see God's glory.

In conclusion, I remain persuaded that revivalism is as important a mechanism for making a people ready for the Lord as it was in the Scriptures and for the founding leaders of the Church of the Nazarene. The optimism of what God could do through Christ to restore his creation led many to hold revivals to call people to return to God (the remnant), to desire a deeper relationship with God (entire sanctification), or to enter into a relationship with God (embrace the call to live as the image of God in the world).

God calls us to be like John the Baptist—to prepare a people and make them ready for the Lord. But we need to be willing to discern how he wants us to prepare his people in our context. For John Wesley, this call included being bold to challenge systemic evil while at the same time calling people to a deeper relationship with God. For Phineas Bresee, it included bringing the marginalized into becoming part of the kingdom of God, even when others in society and the church may have thought that nothing good could come from such people. It also included advocating against systems that result in self-destructive behaviors.

Overall, the Old Testament, the New Testament, John Wesley, Phineas Bresee, and many others of our tradition have affirmed that being prepared for the Lord means having a willingness to embrace a call to love God and others in ways that can only be derived from God's holiness. Our theological forerunners have been willing to interpret God's Word in soteriological ways to address with boldness the sin that so easily entangles. Just as John Wesley, Phineas Bresee, and our biblical ancestors found, reflecting God's holiness in the world will bring about the restoration of God's righteousness in the lives of people who, through our lifestyle and witness, come to see God's salvation or God's glory. I pray that as a church we will always make room for spiritual revival.[4]

I am persuaded that revival is one of God's mechanisms to form his people into his image and likeness. He wants to make us holy and send us out to represent him and his holiness, and he calls us to draw near in repentance: "If my people, who are called by my name, will humble themselves and pray and seek my face and turn from their wicked ways, then I will hear from heaven, and I will forgive their sin and will heal their land" (2 Chron. 7:14).

May the purifying fire of the Holy Spirit burn deep into the hearts and lives of the people called Nazarenes, sanctifying us and emboldening us to continually proclaim the message of holiness with

---

4. Stephane Tibi offers a helpful interpretation of the word "revival," which I apply to this reflection on preparedness for the coming of the Lord. Revival is a word composed of two parts: "re" and "vival." (A) "Re-" stresses a coming back, like in the words "return" or "repent." This is why the term "revive" in the Bible is sometimes a translation of the Hebrew verb *shouv* (שׁוּב), "to return from exile" or "to repent." This reminds us that we have often wandered away from God's purpose and desire for us as humans, as children of God called to eternal communion with our heavenly Father. This touch of eternity is what makes our lives worth living, peaceful, and joyful. (B) "-vival" comes from the Latin root *vivere*, "to live." The verb "revive" in the Bible is also sometimes a translation of the Hebrew verb *hayah* (הָיָה), often translated "to live" or "to be."

our neighbors near and far, despite obstacles and difficulties. The world needs to know that sin's power can be defeated: "Sin needs no longer reign in the heart. An outpouring of God's love into the heart 'excludes sin.' We can live truly holy lives."[5] Let us continue to be faithful to make ready a people prepared for the Lord.

---

5. Leclerc, *Discovering Christian Holiness.*

4
WHY HAVE A RIGHT HEART?
A Wesleyan Middle Way as the Way Forward for Holiness Ethics
DIANE LECLERC

∾

We continue to probe the question "why holiness?" in this chapter. Besides all the possible answers to this question, it should be clear that, at least historically, it is the message to which we are called. John Wesley believed that God raised up the Methodists in an extraordinary way to spread the truth of holiness. The same can be said of the denominations that sprang forth from the Holiness Movement of the nineteenth century. But now that more than a century has passed, some are struggling anew with our identity and purpose. Why holiness? In the spirit of Wesley and those who followed him, it is the message with which God seems to have entrusted us, and we lose our way when we lose that sense of purpose. I would like to suggest, first, that the essence of our holiness message is something that the universal church desperately needs now. But, if we are to remain relevant, our holiness ethic needs revisioning for the sake of the world, the worldwide church, and perhaps, especially right now, for our own people as we move into the future to which God has called us. This chapter will focus on a means of personal and corporate renewal: *orthokardia*—literally meaning a "right heart."

If we were to poll the general population today about some of the perplexities of life, it would probably not take long to land on concerns about the widening polarization between countries of the world, and even between citizens within those countries. For example, in the United States, the polarization is most noticeable in the growing gap between the Democrats' and Republicans' political agendas. Pundits have identified the collapse of the moderate position. Where once moderates were most appealing to the majority of the population, and thus most electable, moderation is now perceived from both the right and the left as weakness, and what would have once been known as extremist ideas are finding the largest followings. Presently, American citizens now vote and hope that their preferred extreme will prevail rather than seeking commonalities or compromise.

This example of a polarity in politics certainly reflects polarization of a deeper kind—dramatically different ideas about what we most value. People are polarized in their underpinning ideologies, and even in what might be called their philosophies of life, or worldviews. We might even argue that political and ideological devotion in different parts of the world has reached the point of mimicking religious sentiment, a situation that alarmed us in the past in various forms (e.g., Nazi ideology), when one's ultimate concern or faith was placed in something other than God; one theologian calls this the demonic.[1]

But before we blame the problems of polarization and extremism on the secularization of culture, we must recognize that the church is not immune. Christianity is in crisis, certainly for a whole host of reasons, but also because we are on the verge of losing a coherent center as we define our theological positions over-against opposing views. Again, using the United States as an example, Christianity

---

1. See Paul Tillich's *Dynamics of Faith* (New York: HarperCollins, 1958).

on the left is now so dissimilar to Christianity on the right that it is probably more appropriate to talk about American Christianities plural, or even two different religions. This polarization represents different orthodoxies and different orthopraxies. In Wesley's words, we no longer "think alike" or "act alike," to such a degree that any essential commonalities of the (creedal) past have vaporized.[2] For example, left-leaning theology often denies the divinity of Christ and his bodily resurrection, and right-leaning theology has reduced Christian faith to a litmus test of fundamentals and made the Bible into an idol.

All of this brings me to this pressing question: Will the Church of the Nazarene and other holiness denominations be able to weather the storms of cultural polarization in our renewed search for our own identity? Or maybe even more importantly in the grand scheme, can we reclaim the *via media* (middle way) of Wesleyanism for the sake of Christianity itself? With the potential split of United Methodism fast approaching over a cultural issue (with moral implications), the holiness tradition is now perhaps uniquely positioned to identify and maintain a Christian center.

Not only do the poles believe differently and act differently, but they also tend to value either belief *or* practice over the other. Certainly to overstate the point, "right belief" (propositional statements) dictates one side while "right action" (social justice) dominates the other. To state the question clearly, what is most important: orthodoxy or orthopraxy? In order to represent the center, we would do well to answer the question about what matters most by answering both: right belief and right practice are equally important! We should hold in tension both orthodoxy and orthopraxy as crucial aspects of Christian faith. Yet we have had great difficulty managing this tension among ourselves of late. And that difficulty is starting to show.

To overstate the point for the sake of making the point, in our denomination we can see the disintegration of the center along genera-

---

2. See John Wesley's sermon "Catholic Spirit."

tional lines. Allow me to generalize. For modern minds, orthodoxy must be preserved at all costs. As anxiety rises and insecurity about the radical changes in the world and in the church becomes a felt need, the tendency is to calcify doctrine: to hold fast to what we have "always" believed becomes paramount. The greatest threat is perceived heresy. But "truth," even as it is "in Jesus," can become rigid, even fossilized. Further, there is a right way to believe about what we practice: specifically, there are strong beliefs about what we *should not* do.

For postmodern minds, orthopraxy is "where it's at!" Postmodern thinkers have been raised in a culture that implicitly instills ideological and moral relativism—thus, what matters most is what we do. Theology and doctrine matter little—or, at the very least, are quite fluid. As a result, we now see little denominational loyalty in these generations because a particular theological position has become practically irrelevant. If we do keep this generation in our church, it is because they strongly identify with the social vision of the Holiness Movement and early Nazarenes. Their practices are directed toward the same social classes John Wesley and Phineas Bresee cared most about. They resonate strongly with the idea that, if theology is to be valid, it must work in real life and address actual situations. Truth is found in what Jesus did among the oppressed. There are strong beliefs about what we *should* do, but there can be a lack of theological depth that makes them incapable of critical analysis of culture and, perhaps, incapable of *sustainable* motivation for action. (Again, forgive the generalizations here.)

One approach to the situation in which we find ourselves could be to tell modern thinkers that they must do a better job at acting rightly by acting socially and the postmodern thinkers that they must do a better job at believing rightly, particularly about sacred doctrines like entire sanctification—trying to bring a balance in the force of our message. But there is another way toward a balancing center—one that comes from our past but is highly pertinent to our future. The emphasis of the Church of the Nazarene in the days to come must be on a renewal of Wesley's convictions about *orthokardia*—right-heart-edness—as the very means toward vital holiness ethics.

A Right Heart: *Orthokardia*

In Wesley's rather famous sermon "Catholic Spirit," he suggests that there is a peculiar love we owe to our fellow brothers and sisters in Christ. However, this love is often hindered by the fact that we do not all "think alike," and we do not all "act alike." It is appropriate to interpret Wesley's meaning here to mean that in non-essentials there can be great diversity of thought. (He seems not to fathom that there could be disagreements about the essentials!) Acknowledging Christian diversity is also to acknowledge the following advice to think and let think:

> Although every person necessarily believes that every particular opinion which he holds is true (for to believe an opinion is not true is the same thing as to not hold it), yet can no one be assured that all of his opinions, taken together are true. . . . Every wise person, therefore, will allow others the same liberty of thinking which he desires they should allow him; and will no more insist on their embracing his opinion than he would have them insist on his embracing theirs. He bears with those who differ from him and only asks, "Is your heart right?"[3]

Wesley also wants us to embrace others who do not act like us. The context of the sermon reveals that Wesley acknowledges here that we do not all worship alike. About 250 years before the modern "worship wars," Wesley suggests that there should be an ability on the part of the loving Christian to "worship and let worship."

In the midst of Wesley's discussion, it becomes key to offer a definition of what it means to have a right heart. Here are Wesley's criteria, in six points:

---

3. Wesley, Sermon 39: "Catholic Spirit," The Wesley Center Online, http://wesley.nnu.edu/john-wesley/the-sermons-of-john-wesley-1872-edition/sermon-39-catholic-spirit/.

1. Do you believe in God? In his wisdom, power, justice, mercy, and truth? Do you walk by faith and not by sight?
2. Do you believe in Jesus Christ, and are you found in him?
3. Is your faith filled with the energy of love? Has love for God cast out love for the world?
4. Are you doing the will of God with an attitude of "not my will, but thine be done?"
5. Is your heart right toward your neighbor? Do you love your enemies?
6. Do you show your love by your works?[4]

Are these doctrinal statements or behavioral statements? The answer is yes! They have theological implications about what we are to believe as Christians, and they have practical implications about how we are to live as Christians. For Wesley, these express the goals and the means of *orthokardia*—these beliefs, actions, and affections flow from a right-hearted person. A word or two on Wesley's understanding of affections will aid us here.

Prior to Wesley's century, Anglicanism was greatly influenced by what is known as the intellectualist model of ethical theory. This theory suggested that reason should be the superior human attribute in all decisions about morality, with the passions (or emotions) as something to fight. Here we would find Plato's idea that to *know* the good is to do the good. Thus, acting wrongly, or "sinning," is a matter of ignorance only. Ethics flows from right reason. However, as empiricism gained in popularity, so did the idea that emotions (or "affections") are also extremely important to any internal motivation to act ethically. "This emphasis on the indispensable contribution of the affections to human action was not limited to philosophers in eighteenth-century England. It found strong advocates as well among theologians seeking to counteract the emerging deistic reduc-

---

4. Wesley, "Catholic Spirit."

tions of religion."[5] This change away from the intellectualist model found great approval by Wesley.

Wesley developed a "moral psychology" that included the vital place of affections. His list of elements in the human being as related to ethical behavior included the will, understanding, liberty, conscience, and certainly the heart. A crucial distinction from an intellectualist model is what Wesley meant by "the will." Wesley believed that the will was influenced not only by reason but also by the affections—perhaps *only* by the affections. In other words, willing was more a function of affections that reside in the heart than an act of "rational self-determination."[6] What did Wesley mean by the word "affections?"

Affections are made up of motivating inclinations rather than just emotions. We act out of our affections. In addition, theologically speaking, they are influenced by outside causes, most particularly by grace. Wesley did not stop there, however. He believed that the affections are habituated into enduring dispositions, which he called "tempers." We act out of these habituated and grace-filled dispositions. In other words, we act out of right-heartedness. The best example of a temper for Wesley was love for God and neighbor. When love fills the heart, this holy temper becomes holy action, at times expressing itself in the negation of something for the sake of the other but most often as positive, loving action. We act lovingly because our hearts are inclined to love.

A Full Heart: *Plaeromakardia*

In order to define further the meaning of right-heartedness for us holiness folks, I will offer a description of what it means to be full-hearted. Very often we have missed it here. In fact, we actually have wrongly emphasized an "empty-heartedness." Let me explain.

---

5. Randy Maddox, "Holiness of Heart and Life: Lessons from North American Methodism," *Asbury Theological Journal* 51, no. 1 (1996), 152–53.

6. Maddox, "Holiness of Heart," 153.

The opposite
of sin is
not
sinlessness.

Mildred Bangs Wynkoop has a rather simple idea that has profound and wide-reaching implications. I will use my own words to describe it. The opposite of sin is not sinlessness. One cannot understand the nature of something by only referencing a vacuum, a black hole, an absence of something else. And yet, in the more legalistic periods in Nazarene history, holiness as the opposite of sin *was* defined as sinlessness. The imperative goal was to rid one's life of sins of commission. I am not saying that this is unimportant—there is an element of sanctifying grace that purifies our hearts. But if we stop here, our theology actually becomes dangerous. It implies that personal piety is the end goal of the sanctified life. The focus is on the things we should not do, but we can forget *why* we do not do them.

Say you want to run a marathon and you begin to train. You are building stamina and improving the time it takes to finish. The goals are endurance and speed. But there is a problem. Each time before you run, you eat five cheeseburgers. What would happen to your endurance and your time? Let it suffice to say that it would not be pretty. And so you determine that you will *not* eat the five cheeseburgers, and eventually you stop eating any cheeseburgers at all. You say to yourself, "Thou shalt not eat cheeseburgers." Your entire focus becomes what you do not eat. But in this focused determination, you eventually forget that the original goal was to run a marathon. You are content with what you do not do, and sit sedentarily.

At times in our history, we have forgotten the true goal of the sanctified life and have only focused on the "thou shalt nots." It is true that to do something, there are things we must not do. To run a marathon, we really shouldn't eat five cheeseburgers before every training run. But it has been too easy to focus on what we should not do in order to pursue holiness to such a degree that we forget *why* we do not do things. A sinless heart is not necessarily a holy heart.

To put it in Wynkoop's frame, we have only defined holiness as the absence of sin. Jesus tells a small but powerful parable in Luke 11:24–26: "When an impure spirit comes out of a person, it goes through arid places seeking rest and does not find it. Then it says,

'I will return to the house I left.' When it arrives, it finds the house swept clean and put in order. Then it goes and takes seven other spirits more wicked than itself, and they go in and live there. And the final condition of that person is worse than the first." If a house is swept clean without something to replace the evil spirit, it remains vulnerable. Holiness is not just the absence of sin but the presence of love. A right heart, then, is a full heart—a heart full of love, brought by the indwelling presence of the Holy Spirit. The full heart, then, acts lovingly.

Further, according to John Wesley, love is the very means by which sin is removed. His simple phrase "love excluding sin" should speak volumes to us. The sanctified heart is a heart full of love; the heart is so full of the love of God that sin is pushed out. That love takes up the full capacity of the heart so that sin can no longer reign and, eventually, no longer remain. It is then out of a heart of love (or character of love) that we act lovingly. Wesley transcends the faith/works dialectic by asking such questions as, "Is your faith filled with the energy of love?"

And so, a full heart is full of love. But a full heart—a sanctified heart, if you will—also contains the right motivations for action. Aristotle elaborates on four types of character that potentially emerge from a tension between knowing and doing. First, there is the "**vicious**" character. In this instance, the person knows what he or she ought to do but chooses to do otherwise, with no remorse. The "**incontinent**" character describes the person who knows what ought to be done, chooses in fact to do it, but then fails to follow through and does not act in the way decided upon. The "**continent**" character is closer to the ideal but misses it because of motivation. This character knows the good and does the good, but only out of duty. Each of the three characters described above evidences some lack of internal harmony. The harmonious life only comes to those with **"virtuous"** character. The truly virtuous character knows the good and does the good for the sake of virtue itself, not out of the internal pressure of guilt or the external pressure of a fear of punishment or even a promise of reward. The virtuous person acts in complete harmony with the knowledge he or she possesses, out of an internal temper or desire for good, for good's sake.

And so, our motivation matters to our character. We find this in Wesley's discussion of purity of intentions. Sanctification affects our intentions. But if we are honest, we must admit that many Nazarenes have been stuck in continent character, living their lives out of a sense of duty. We know there is so much more to life than this. The ultimate goal is to have, and live out of, a heart like Christ's.

Christ's Heart: *Christokardia*

On the night that Jesus was betrayed, he took a towel and basin and washed his disciples' feet. The writer of the Gospel interjects that in so doing, "he loved them to the end" (John 13:1). We know that Jesus took the position of a slave in this act. Often this description is used to highlight the servanthood of Jesus. And, as Peter's question to Jesus suggests (v. 6), this act of humility is supposedly not appropriate for a Messiah. Nevertheless, this act of humility bridges foot washing to the submission at Gethsemane, to the trial, and to the cross. Jesus could have lorded it over his disciples, said no in the garden, pleaded his case at trial, fought back at his scourging, and rejected the cross. But Jesus died. Jesus, the fully divine and fully human one, died a real, human death.

There is great significance in the fact that Jesus, with deep and pervasive humility, became obedient to death, even death on a cross. Jesus underwent the totality of the human experience through to its end. This was the truest expression of the extent of his love—that Jesus emptied himself, laid down his life for his friends, and was entombed. Moreover, it must not be forgotten that he died on a cross—the most graphic and elucidatory symbol of guilt and shame in that culture. He died the most humiliating death imaginable.

"Whoever wants to be my disciple must deny themselves and take up their cross daily and follow me. For whoever wants to save their life will lose it, but whoever loses their life for me will save it"

(Luke 9:23–24). These verses are extremely familiar to us as holiness people who believe that consecration and surrender are the very means to entire sanctification. Yet, while we are experts at self-denial (experts at all those "thou shalt nots"), we have not always understood the call to pick up our crosses. We have interpreted it to mean that we have a cross to carry from time to time—an illness to bear or some period of personal struggle. We forget that Jesus's cross was a complete and final sacrifice for the other. Therefore, we take up our crosses when we suffer on behalf of *others*! Further, we misunderstand Jesus if we lose our lives *in order to* save ourselves. Securing our own salvation is a result, not a motivation. Presupposing a Christocentric faith, the call is to pour out our hearts and our lives as Christ poured out his—on behalf of those who cannot save themselves.

This is not a political agenda—it is the biblical mandate. Like Christ, we are called to feed the hungry, clothe the naked, heal the sick, give sight to the blind, let the oppressed go free, and proclaim the year of the Lord. The biblical mandate leads us to fight injustice, resist any disregard of human dignity, and perhaps work against public policy that stands against the marginalized. I would propose that we will understand these things more deeply, and we will be able to discern the ethics of Christian action, when our orthodoxy is Christocentric and when our orthopraxy is truly Christlike. The Wesleyan revival in Great Britain and the early Holiness Movement in America seemed to understand these things. And the early Nazarenes seemed to embody these things. They knew what to believe, and they knew what to do because their hearts were right, and full—a reflection of the heart of Jesus.

Only with love at the center of our hearts are we ever enabled to reflect the holy God and to be holy as God is holy. Rob Staples, speaking on love in a presentation titled "Things Shakeable and Things Unshakeable in Holiness Theology," concludes:

> I would want to say that the love that is the "core distinctive" of holiness is the love of the crucified God! It is the kenotic divine love of the suffering Servant who, says Isaiah, "poured out

Only with love at the center of our hearts are we ever enabled to reflect the holy God and to be holy as God is holy.

his soul unto death" (Isa. 53:12, KJV). It is the self-denying, cross-bearing love of Matthew 16:24. It is the love depicted by Dietrich Bonhoeffer who said: "When Jesus calls a man to follow him, he bids him come and die." It is the love of the lowly Galilean, washing the feet of his followers, emptying himself, making himself of no reputation, taking the form of a servant, and becoming obedient even to death on a cross. The love that is the core distinctive of holiness is a cruciform love. It is the love described so graphically in the fifteenth chapter of Luke: a love that goes out into the darkness of night, searching amid the hills and valleys, among the briars and the brambles, looking for that one lost sheep; a love that looks in every corner, sweeping in every nook and cranny, searching for that one lost coin; a love that stands forever out by the gatepost gazing yearningly, longingly, down the long road that leads in from the far country. That is love . . . That is holiness! That is what Wesleyan [Holiness] Theology calls "perfect love." That cannot be shaken.[7]

This type of Christlike, cruciform love keeps our beliefs from becoming calcified and dead. It leads to a type of "generous" orthodoxy on non-essentials, also called "catholic spirit." This type of love keeps our orthopraxy focused on God's telos for every human being, which could be called teleological orthopraxy, or soteriological justice. And this type of *orthokardia* love is the way forward to any vital discussion of holiness ethics or Christian action for today and in the future, as we allow our faith to be filled with the energy of love.

---

7. Rob Staples, "Things Shakeable and Things Unshakeable in Holiness Theology," The Edwin Crawford Lecture, Northwest Nazarene University's Wesley Conference: *Revisioning Holiness*, February 9, 2007. See nnu.edu/Wesley.

5
WHY ENGAGE THE MARGINS?

The Practical Applications of Holiness in the Life of the Church

DEIRDRE BROWER LATZ

൭൦

For Christians in the holiness tradition, our ultimate goal is entire sanctification—a sense of complete and total love for God saturating the soul, body, mind, and heart. This love is an all-consuming deep relationship between God and us that is sealed, eternal, truthful, and dynamic. Throughout many centuries, Christians have revealed this type of love by living saintly, prayerful lives—hearing God's voice both aloud and through Scripture—and being responsive to God's direction. This love is personal, deep, and very good.

Because of God's love, Christians from all backgrounds have made a direct translation of Christian conversion into faith toward belonging, participating, and engaging alongside others in what we call the church. The church is Christ's body—a corporate gathering that reflects something of the nature of God. It is a holy community of holy people who are called to live out faith alongside each other.

True holiness is both deeply personal and interpersonal.

It is a drawing together of people who, in unity and love, (should) demonstrate something of God's love at work. The church, as a holy people of God, reflects the nature of God and lives out God's love in the wider world.

A community of holy people can do different things with their holiness. A temptation has been to be an inward-looking community, preserving their holiness *against* others, clearly defining boundaries of what holiness looks, acts, and sounds like. This kind of holiness is narrow and sectarian (like the Pharisees). Sometimes, a temptation has been individualistic, extremely pietistic, where the holiness is purely a matter of inner holiness and the only judge is God and one-self. This means that the community is little more than a gathering of people with competing viewpoints, accountable for neither their lives nor their hearts. If they can justify what they do before God, on their own terms, they can accommodate God to their own views (like Apollo or Judas).

Of course, the *truest* expression of holy community is represented for us in the messy text of Scripture that shows us that a relationship with God, in Christ—true holiness—is both deeply personal and in-terpersonal. Such a community is always structured around prayer, food, worship, song, *and in* the care of the weakest, the widows, the orphans, the least of these, and the children. In example after exam-ple, we see that lives are transformed by God's loving mercy. Think of the lepers, the haemorrhaging women, the Samaritan men—the wider community touched by the contagious love God has for us and for all people. This outworking of holy love is profoundly just and truly practical. This is the truest expression of church—belonging to God and one another and seeking to be so Godward that God's love infuses the heart, touches the soul, and gives strength to the body. The impulse of this kind of love is to share it with others.

Such love tugs Christians to be outward facing, not only in de-claring God's love but also in enacting it. Outward-facing love means the community learns to be planted and rooted and acts out love in creative, compassionate, transformative ways. This kind of love engages in mercy that cradles the broken, lifts the fallen, embraces the found, restores the lonely, renews life for the dying, and gives water to the thirsty. This is active holiness, spurred on by gathering together and dispersed out into real life. Once in touch with real life, active holiness does more than act well; it also engages in compassion that brings about renewal and transformation in individuals and communities.

The truth is that, very often, we holiness people have been good at seeking to serve others: we have habitually acted out love in lots of practical ways. We have engaged in thinking about how to offer a cup of water, or the contemporary equivalent, and we have tried to do so over time. The challenge to our holy communities is not just to act rightly but also to broaden our scope and engage in shaping the world around us more justly. This will look different in different places and communities, but there are a number of core ideas that we can embrace that will shape such lives. These ideas are rooted in holiness and in the virtues of loving God and loving others as ourselves as the greatest commands flow from us into action. Some of these ways involve *thinking* about the way we approach the world around us, and some involve *acting* in new ways, or rediscovering some older ways of being just.

Dignity

One of the ways we see justice working itself out as a holy community is in how people treat one another, not just within the community or congregation but in all human interaction. The question at the heart of this is, "If this person were Jesus, how would I treat them?" This means looking past the easiest and most obvious label we might give a person (whether rich or poor, ugly or beautiful, clean or dirty) and remembering that *this* person is created in God's image and can be brought—by God's love, mercy, and the power of the Holy Spirit—to Christlikeness by a miracle of grace. Imagine if each person we met were seen and treated by each one of us as infinitely worthy, for in them we would meet Christ. Imagine if we understood each person as truly worthy of Christ's love. In that moment, things that create barriers socially or culturally would be reduced as if to nothing, and the truest reality of that person's being would be laid out before us.

Seeing through these eyes means that we treat the sinner as the guest and the saint as the companion in hosting the feast. If biblical examples are helpful, we see this kind of thinking in the Old Testament's requirements to care for the alien, the widow, the orphan, and the poor, and in the New Testament in the way Jesus is with people—from the adulterous woman to the extravagant perfume pourer, from the scenes with tax collectors to the Last Supper, where he eats with his betrayer. God, in Christ, loves people, although certainly we are gripped by sin and brokenness. If we take this love seriously, then practical actions—such as learning people's names and stories, touching them with dignity, and asking questions rather than making assumptions—enable justice to creep into our presence.

Attentiveness

Love in the general sense is not the whole story of holy people working out justice. A further framing of our thinking is in being attentive to a person's entire story and to their life in community. A question here might be, "What is being said through what is being done?" It's difficult to be attentive in a culture saturated with social media and short on time and space to listen well. For many of us, the idea of being attentive is a hard stretch because we are busy, but if we attend well, we may discover that the world is complex and that the people we encounter experience injustice in multiple ways. For example, we volunteer at a food bank and wonder why a particular woman is there to get food for her family. When we attend to her story, we discover that her husband lost his job and that the loss of his dignity means he drinks. His drinking uses the household income in destructive ways. He hates himself. His children fear him. His wife holds the home together. But then we look at the wider story. His job is one of hundreds lost locally due to corporate takeovers and technological changes. His anger at this loss leads to his actions. His actions bring about destruction. His destruction has wider social effects beyond his own family; his children and wife, their neighbours, and the community all have a pall of death. Understanding this story, attending to it in all of its breadth and depth, is part of the practice of justice.

Wesley has some great lines here, which I will paraphrase. In one place he talks about a poor woman and argues that the only way we can understand that she hasn't created her own poverty is by seeing for ourselves how hard she works and seeing that she's desperately poor anyway. He argues that being with people like this is part of our holy living. This is practicing attentiveness and, of course, takes time. It's not client-based or by rote; it's not easy, quick, or task-oriented. Being attentive requires us to listen closely to our neighbours' stories, again and again.

Of course, we are also to be attentive to our own roles here, our own assumptions, prejudices, and cultural norms. Maybe we need to learn to value the world around us differently and to see that the immense power of the woman holding her family together is worthy of utmost respect. Maybe we need to interrogate and be attentive to our own responses to this man and the lessons of his life. Maybe we need to reconsider and be attentive to our own participation in supporting unjust systems, or in the way we so easily slip into treating people as our culture does—looking down on poor people, blaming them for their situation, or assuming that nothing can be changed. This attentiveness to our own assumptions might lead us to a conversion of sorts, from assuming we know to discovering God's doing something new in these moments. A biblical example of this might be the story of Peter, when God reveals that the old food taboos are going to be broken down (Acts 10:9–16). Peter's cultural frame of reference is pulled apart by God's desire to get the message of good news to the gentiles. Being attentive to God's voice reshaping us is profoundly practical—and humbling.

A further attentiveness is also paying attention to the ways in which fractured lives are shaped by systems and structures that allow oppression or injustice to reign. This is partly how the principalities and powers seem to work. So we attend to the places in our own cultures where things are out of step with God's desires for wholeness and peace. Attending to these places might take us into the arenas of politics or the marketplace, industry or medicine, science or entertainment, education or the media. In these spheres the complex web of justice impacts the church, since we are people who live real lives in the ordinary world. Attending to the injustices around us is vital. It takes a willingness to be connected to the world God loves and to discover those places where sin and death are at work, but in faith and with love, we can attend to it in hope of transforming the world for God's sake.

Participation

So we treat people with dignity—that is holy. We attend to their story—that is holy. And we often respond—deeply and compassionately. The church's response has often been to give the woman food. That is good. Often this is accompanied by spiritual succour. That is also good. We look beyond the individual story to the wider and more complex realities and name that which is not of God and attend to it. But, as holy people, following the ways of our holy God, mirroring Christ's approach to people he loves, we also are called to be active participants in restoring the well-being of the wider family, community, and world around us. We participate, and we enable others to participate, in living lives well, in peaceful coexistence—or, shalom. Shalom and justice are bedfellows; they kiss each other. The whole idea of being in Christ as a participant in Christ's life embodied in the world is powerful. It changes us wholly. But it also intentionally joins others in enabling them to participate in the restoration of their own community.

This idea calls us to ask wider questions such as, "What if we broadened our attention to consider job creation, local educational support, addiction support groups, and social enterprises that help local families transform their own lives?" Or, "What if we joined to advocate for businesses to develop in our community?" These powerful questions ensure participation in restoration—not as power brokers but as ambassadors of the kingdom.

The idea that we share in the transformation of people's lives by participating alongside them in rewriting their own stories is a guard against thinking of ourselves as the Messiah and a way of putting salvation in the right place—a gift from God for all people. Humanising people, giving people their own voice and receiving the truths they have to share, is a powerful witness of grace.[1] The idea of being *for* people is important, but participation means that we are called to be *with* people. In this way, we come alongside one another in shaping communities for justice as a practice of being a holy community.

Voice

One of the ways holiness is expressed is almost always in the transformation of voice, from violent cursing to sacred song. So, a people who were once not a people are given songs of praise, magnification, lament, sorrow, and joy. This is not just a new voice directed to God, though. Holy people who are engaged in practices of justice will be willing to join in declaring hope, speaking God's vision, preaching in a different way, and ushering in the kingdom. These ways are marked by ceasing oppression, releasing captives, using right weights, building straight roads, digging deep wells, and harvesting from fields that bear good grain, with the edges left for the sustenance of widows and orphans. Practicing mercy and justice is a model for us of God's intent: the least of these receive care as if they were Christ.

---

1. There is a wonderful example of some of this through "poverty truth commissions," wherein active Christian participation has led to people from the poorest communities being heard, valued, considered, and empowered. You can see this here: http://www.leedspovertytruth.org.uk.

Justice is a slow process that involves courageously unpacking many of our own religious assumptions.

The idea of voice being attached to how we live out our holiness as a people is that we declare alongside each other what is true of God and what God desires for people, for their lives, and for their communities. A good example is in the anti-human-trafficking movements we Nazarenes are aligned with. Another is in our statements against violence to women and men, or voicing together that we abhor racism in any and all forms. The voicing of God's loving compassion reflects Jesus's ways: speaking in tenderness to some and confrontation to others; casting out demons from some and asking others if they want to be made well; naming disciples and calling people to a different future of following him rather than their old ways. Here we ask, "What is God saying?" and "What would God have *me* say?"

Voice in this sense is speaking *with, for, alongside,* and *to.* When we speak *with* people, we enable their voices to be heard. We speak *for* people when the voices of others need to be amplified. We speak *alongside* people with shared outrage at injustice (even if we speak from different starting points) and speak *to* power, whether in the structures of the civic society or the church. The role of the holiness community as a right-speaking, truth-telling group gives impetus to a growing reputation that God is for people and that God's love can be seen in justice breaking through. Such a way of holiness is in keeping with God, who hears the cry of the oppressed and sends spokespeople among them to speak freedom to them.

The More Difficult Way

Justice is a slow process that involves courageously unpacking many of our own religious assumptions. If we take seriously that we must keep our eyes wide and ears open to be truly attentive to what the world around us is actually saying, we might find that there's work to be done that transforms us as well as those with whom we live and alongside whom we work. Then we can move from holy *sectarian* community to holy community in a beautiful and dynamic pattern of growth that demonstrates God's working in and through us. For instance, if we attend to the broken places and spaces in our wider communities, we may realise that staying put or moving back in is truly just, though inconvenient. We may discover that some of our modes of behavior, such as solving problems for people, only create limping communities, not walking ones. We may find out that we are part of structures or systems of injustice and that we perpetuate some cycles unwittingly that ensure broken people feel less than dignified in our presence. We might notice that even when people respond to the gospel it is only skin deep because the at-the-root injustices they experience have not been changed. When this happens, cycles that Christ *can* break are not broken because we've not gone far to ensure that people become active agents and participants in the kingdom purposes of God that enable change in individuals and whole communities to take place.

This is difficult. Living in a place and changing it over time—moving in, being present—is culturally challenging. This is difficult because in many of our countries, we have recreated a pernicious individualism, a dualism between matter and spirit—saving souls but not bodies. This is difficult because in some places we are below the radar, only meeting in house groups and meeting in fear of our lives. This is difficult—but it is necessary.

The truth of holiness meeting justice is that it reveals something of our deepest reality: are we only aligned to God in our worship and prayer, a heavenly direction, upwardly? Or, is loving others as ourselves reshaping us into a holy community that has dared to embark on God's mission? Are we holy in a narrow way, or are we bravely holy, trusting that the transformation of entire communities of people can happen when the wildness of God is at work? Justice is brave, takes risks, is contagious, restores to right places, and is a powerful witness to God's self-giving love. Those whose holiness leads them to just living also discover that they learn something of the wideness of God's grace. These ideas (and others) shape congregations into brave communities that change the world.

The practical outworking of this might be very *ordinary*, such as a church that determines to encourage holiness through not overeating but by joining in a congregational fast, or a congregation that determines that they will become known as an open-door gathering place for prisoners just leaving jail. It might look like campaigns to stop raw sewage from being dumped in the local stream, or a congregation that adopts abandoned babies and then advocates for better HIV medication for mothers so babies aren't orphaned anymore. It might mean a congregation that helps reclaim the mountain by planting trees and stopping mudslides, or a congregation that pays for a mental health specialist for the local community based in the church. It might look like a congregation that works with other local churches to shelter street people throughout the winter and calls them guests, welcoming them as if they were staying in a hotel. It might look like a congregation that pools their resources to pay for funerals for elderly people who die alone, or a congregation that sets up a cleaning and cooking rotation for the mother who has breast cancer so she can spend her energy playing with her kids. All of these real-life examples are holy, local responses to the lived realities of particular communities. While they may not be applicable in every context, this is the nature of holiness in community that works toward justice. It is powerful, it is beautiful, it loves, it is wholly good, and it is wholly God.

6

WHY PRACTICE HOLINESS IN THE WILDERNESS?

Contemporary Expressions of Holiness

DANNY QUANSTROM

༄

Do you remember "the good old days?" The satirical website *The Onion* traces "the good old days" back to the weekend of June 19, 1948. They write, "After extensive interviews, analysis of personal correspondence, and repeated viewings of that week's *Ed Sullivan Show*, we have pinpointed the precise time period this phrase signifies."[1] Do you remember that weekend?

This blatantly satirical article reveals two truths: First, the power of nostalgia is strong, and while most of us don't remember anything at all about that particular day, I'm guessing something pops up in your mind when you read the phrase "the good old days." For some of us, this phrase evokes high school or college memories. Others might think of the early days in their marriage or the weekends camping with their young children. The thing about "the good old

---

1. "'Good Old Days' Traced Back to Single Weekend in 1948," *The Onion*, https://www.theonion.com/good-old-days-traced-back-to-single-weekend-in -1948-1819571809.

days" is that they were rarely even that good. We rarely reminisce about that one weekend when we slept in until noon, ate Cheetos for lunch, and binge-watched our favorite TV shows. Those are the times we forget. Instead, we remember the two-a-day practices for high school cheerleading, the late-night drama rehearsals charged up by soda or energy drinks, or the all-night study sessions with good friends over bad coffee. We rarely remember life's easy moments, but we can't forget the challenging times. Often, those challenging times become "the good old days."

The other thing this silly article reveals is that things aren't the way they used to be. Those of us who were alive in 1948 likely remember a time when a household *might* have one television or *one* vehicle, a time when "organic" wasn't a *thing*, a time without cable, internet, smartphones, or social media. When I reflect on my grandparents' generation, I am struck by how gracefully they've handled this rapidly changing world. Think about it. Few generations in human history have experienced as much societal, cultural, or technological change as members of what has come to be labeled the Greatest Generation. Not only has the geographical landscape changed in the last hundred years, but the social, political, sexual, and even religious landscapes have changed as well.

With the advent of the printing press, Western society and the Western church underwent radical transformation and reformation. Five hundred years after Luther's 95 Theses, we have another new major technological innovation: the internet. Now, other people—not just information—are accessible to the masses. Nearly a decade ago Phyllis Tickle argued that every five hundred years or so, the church has these seismic shifts with new paradigms for a new world.[2] It's not hard to see that the church is operating in a landscape that looks awfully different from the church of the nineteenth or twenti-

---

2. See Phyllis Tickle's *Emergence Christianity: What It Is, Where It Is Going, and Why It Matters* (Grand Rapids: Baker Books, 2012).

eth centuries. If we're honest, we really don't even know where these seismic shifts will lead us. The church today is in uncharted waters.

The Bible has an image for this sense of longing for yesteryear in the midst of a changing landscape: the wilderness. For the Israelites, the wilderness was the time between the times. They were no longer in Egypt but hadn't quite made it to Canaan. For the Israelites, the wilderness story was, perhaps, the most fundamental motif. Walter Brueggemann notes that present scholars place the writing of Exodus during the sixth century BCE.[3] That means the story of the wilderness was written by the exilic (or post-exilic) Israelites. This matters to us today because it reveals that the wilderness story wasn't composed as mere history but had pastoral implications. When the Israelites were in exile in Babylon—the time between the times— they needed to remember the faithfulness of YHWH in a previous time between the times. Exile was merely a new form of wilderness.

In order to discuss contemporary expressions of holiness, it is important to understand our current context, and I contend that the church is currently in a state of wilderness. The church, at least the church in the West, is between the times. This wilderness, however, isn't necessarily geographical, as it was with the Israelites, but cultural. We're moving out of modernity and Christendom, but we're not quite sure where God is taking us; some call it postmodernity while others refuse to even name it yet. We're moving out of a paradigm during which the church stood in a position of prominence and power with cultural influence to a place we haven't yet figured out.

For the people of God in the wilderness, things shifted dramatically. The place they had called home for generations was long gone, the landscape had changed dramatically, and they weren't exactly sure when they were going to arrive, or precisely where YHWH was leading them. For the Israelites, the certainty of slavery was preferred to the uncertainty of the wilderness. When we read Exodus 16 and

---

3. Walter Brueggemann, *The New Interpreter's Bible: Genesis to Leviticus* (Nashville: Abingdon Press, 1994), vol. 1.

God never fulfills
God's promises
by taking the
people back to
former things.

17, we see that the people complained against God because they were hungry and thirsty. In the wilderness, the sources of life looked and felt different—the bread came from bushes, the meat from heaven, and the water from a rock. In the wilderness, the cisterns changed.

What we see in the wilderness is that God never fulfills God's promises by taking the people back to former things. The perennial prophetic call, from Isaiah to John the Revelator is this: "Behold, I am making all things new" (Rev. 21:5, ESV; see also Isa. 43:19). As we move into a time in which things are shifting dramatically, the places we have called home for generations may be long gone. As the landscape shifts, so may our particular expressions of holiness. In one sense, the church is *always* in the wilderness. We are the people who live between the times. We are always a pilgrim people, leaving the former things and sojourning toward the coming kingdom. Could it be, then, that God is *still* taking God's people to new places?

Thus, as the church shifts from the certainty of Christendom and cultural influence to the uncertainty of the wilderness, our imagination will need to shift. Our imagination should be shaped by those sojourning in the wilderness more than it should be shaped by the certainty of former paradigms.

The Passover

A few months ago my wife and I were gifted a special treat by some good friends—a trip to the Chicago production of *Hamilton*. Lin-Manuel Miranda wrote, arguably, this generation's most popular and most important Broadway musical about one of the United States' most obscure founding fathers. The musical tells of a Caribbean immigrant child's journey through King's College (Columbia University today), participation in the American Revolution, extramarital affairs, and the development of what became the Federal Reserve System. What is most striking about *Hamilton* isn't just the story it tells but also the way in which the story is told. Unlike most period pieces, *Hamilton* is blatantly anachronistic; it doesn't seek to tell an eighteenth-century story in eighteenth-century lan-

As holiness is
realized in our lives
by the habits we
form, our habits are
shaped by the
ways in which
we worship.

guage with eighteenth-century outcomes. Rather, this piece tells an eighteenth-century story in twenty-first-century language with twenty-first-century outcomes. Most of *Hamilton* is told through the medium of rap and hip-hop. A few hundred years later, *Hamilton* retells historic events in contemporary language in order to teach us something today.

So it is with Exodus 12. As we've already noted, the Passover story was written not by those who experienced it but by exiled Israelites. Exodus 12 tells an ancient story in sixth-century language with sixth-century outcomes. A few hundred years after the Passover, Exodus 12 retells events in what was then contemporary language in order to teach something in that day. The Israelites in exile needed to remember that YHWH was the God of deliverance and liberty. *Salvation* for those in slavery and for those in exile was liberation from their current oppression. And those in exile didn't just remember the deliverance of YHWH: what we see is that they *practiced* the deliverance of YHWH. Passover was a bit of a performance.

Exodus 12:1–14 gave the people of God particular actions to take, some of which sound pretty strange to us today. Put briefly, the very first month of the Israelite calendar was marked by a family (or two) gathering, slaughtering a lamb, placing the blood on their doorposts, and consuming nearly every part of the slaughtered lamb with unleavened bread and bitter herbs. They did all of this hurriedly, with their staff in hand, loins girded, and sandals on their feet. The Passover meal was a worship ritual whereby the people of God remembered and reenacted YHWH's past deliverance in anticipation of YHWH's future deliverance.

These particular worship elements formed the people in particular ways. First, let's look at the slaughtering of the lamb. Notice that this Paschal lamb wasn't the *sacrificial* lamb or a *scapegoat*; that will appear in Isaiah. The Paschal lamb was to be consumed; it was an actual meal. The slaughtering and eating of the lamb was a reminder of God's provision in challenging times. In an act that sounds barbaric to us, they took the blood and placed it on their doorposts and lintels.

That is, they took the very sign of life and placed it in the most prominent place. The life of this lamb represented for the people of Israel the life of the nation. The lifeblood of the lamb ensured deliverance for the people of God. As a sign of life posted in the most public of places, the blood of the lamb meant that the Destroyer could not enter the household. Finally, they ate hurriedly, with loins girded, staff in hand, and sandals on their feet as a way to practice being ready for deliverance. They needed to be ready to leave at a moment's notice.

For the people of God, the Passover was more than just a meal or something to be watched. The practices of the worship ritual formed within them habits they carried through their daily lives. As the people of God today navigate their way out of modernity toward whatever is coming next, we will need careful reflection on how our worship rituals are shaping us. As holiness is realized in our lives by the habits we form, our habits are shaped by the ways in which we worship. Samuel Wells writes, "The center of the church's life is the *practices* through which the church is formed, extended, and restored."[4] Since the Israelites needed particular worship practices to shape their imaginations and habits as they ventured out into the wilderness, let us consider the rituals present in our worship and how they shape our own imaginations and habits today.

Call to Worship

The Christian has two movements with the world. We will get to the second movement later, but the first movement out of the world is practiced in our call to worship. When we gather for worship we practice being the "called-out ones," the *ekklesia*. In being called out from the world, we are separate and distinct, set apart for God's holy purposes. The holy ones are those who have been set apart from the sin and brokenness of this world, as we read in 1 Peter 2:9–10: "But you are a chosen people, a royal priesthood, a holy nation, God's spe-

---

4. Samuel Wells, *Improvisation: The Drama of Christian Ethics* (Grand Rapids: Brazos Press, 2004).

cial possession, that you may declare the praises of him who called you out of darkness into his wonderful light. Once you were not a people, but now you are the people of God; once you had not received mercy, but now you have received mercy." When we are called to worship, we practice this holy movement of being called out of the world.

Passing of the Peace

In the beginning God created by speaking life into existence. As those created in God's image, our language is never neutral. It is always creating or destroying. Christians in the wilderness may be keenly aware of the voices of violence around us. This is why we need to speak words of peace to one another as often as we can!

The passing of the peace during worship provides an opportunity for Christians to be reconciled to one another as well as shaped by how we greet others outside of worship. As followers of the Prince of Peace, we are to be agents of the peaceable kingdom! We practice this peace during worship when we speak it to one another.

Responsive Reading

While responsive readings may take various forms, the practice of call and response forms in us the way we live out holy lives. A responsive reading at the beginning of a service sets the stage for what that service will be—give and take between the One and the many. As the pastor calls, the people respond. So it is with God and God's people. God is the one calling out, and we are the ones responding. The worship service, then, is a conversation between God and God's people. At times we are listening as God speaks, yet there are also moments when God listens to us.

As much as the responsive reading is practicing what we do in worship, it is also a practice for how holy lives are formed. The life of the believer is one that is always listening to the voice of the Lord and always responding to that voice with thanksgiving, with petition, with intercession, or even with lament. The life of holiness is a life lived in constant conversation with the Lord.

Prayer of Invocation

The prayer of invocation is, truly, a response. We invoke the presence of the Lord, or invite God into our midst, knowing it was God who first invited us into God's presence. The invitation during this prayer is derivative. We can and should invite God into our lives because God has already invited us. This mutual invitation prepares our hearts for worship as a holy practice.

Like the prayer of invocation, holiness is derivative. Christian holiness is not something achieved or guaranteed based on merit. The apostle Peter wrote this when he quoted Leviticus: "But just as he who called you is holy, so be holy in all you do; for it is written: 'Be holy, because I am holy'" (1 Peter 1:15–16). Any holiness in the believer is derived from the holiness of God.

Reading of the Scriptures

The reading of the Scriptures for personal devotional study is not bad or inappropriate, but when we read the Scriptures in corporate worship, we receive them as they were intended—out loud, in public. When we read the Scriptures in worship, we take them out of our control and place ourselves in their control. As Dr. Joe Gorman writes, "Not only do we read scripture, but scripture reads us."[5]

The simple act of listening to Scripture during worship shapes holy habits for Christians. It reminds us that we are neither the focus nor the center of this faith. What's more, neither are the Scriptures! When we read the Bible together, we see that the Bible is only the Word of God inasmuch as it reveals the Word of God to us! The Bible reveals Christ to us. By reading Scripture out loud in worship, Christians practice making Christ the center of our lives. By reading Scripture, we practice listening to the voice of the Lord.

We also have communion with the saints when we read the Bible. By simply reading this text, we give allegiance to Christ's church, for

---

5. *A Plain Account: A Free Online Wesleyan Lectionary Commentary*, http://www.aplainaccount.org/reign-of-christ-a-gospel.

it was the faithful and often painful discernment of the church that handed us our holy Bible. By reading it, we place ourselves under the authority of the church and have fellowship with the saints.

Songs of Praise

There are two particular things holy Christians practice when we sing songs of praise. First, songs of praise teach us about Christ and his church. Sorry, Pastor, but your people learn more theology from the songs they sing than from the sermons they hear. Nothing has really changed from when we learned the alphabet as children: one of the best ways for us to learn is by singing.

Second, perhaps it is no surprise that songs became the topic of our "worship wars" and the primary distinction between our traditional and contemporary services. When music shifts in our worship, it isn't just the style or the substance people miss. There are plenty of contemporary songs with great words that aren't pushing the volume or tempo. The issue is *connection*. Something incredibly special happens within us when the church sings songs of praise to God. Today's temptation is to turn the volume up, the lights down, and produce the snot out of worship songs in the name of congregant comfortability, but do you remember how special it was when the soundboard cut out right in the middle of "Be Thou My Vision" and the church had to finish it a cappella?

When we sing songs of praise with our sisters and brothers, we have a connection not only with God but also with one another. In fact, it's biological! When people sing songs together, their hearts beat in unison to the beat of the music.[6] Bjorn Vickhoff, who studied choirs' heartbeats, found that "the readout from the pulse monitors starts as a jumble of jagged lines, but quickly becomes a series of uniform peaks. The heart rates fall into a shared rhythm guided by

---

6. Anna Haensch, "When Choirs Sing, Many Hearts Beat As One," NPR, https://www.npr.org/sections/health-shots/2013/07/09/200390454/when -choirs-sing-many-hearts-beat-as-one.

the song's tempo."[7] We practice holy unity with sisters and brothers when we sing songs of praise together.

Offering

As much as we'd rather not talk about money during times of worship, if we neglect to give our offerings to the Lord, we may be neglecting a very formative means of grace. The holy Christian gives to the church not merely so that the church can have heat during the winter. As important as that may be, the holy Christian gives to the church to be reminded that what Christians have isn't ours. When we participate in the offering, we cast our lot with the two faithful slaves who took what was entrusted to them and invested it in the kingdom (Matt. 25:14–30). We may never see a return on our offerings, but by giving to Christ's church, we tacitly affirm that there is an economy greater than ours.

We can see, then, that giving out of our resources during worship also forms us to be stewards of all that our Good Father has entrusted to us. Not the least of these good things is creation. The offering reminds us that all we see, all we touch, every person we know, was created by God, and God said it was good. Through the offering, Christians learn the holy act of acknowledging that other people are created in the image of God. Through the offering, Christians learn the holy act of not taking more than is needed. Through the offering, Christians are formed to care for creation.

Corporate Prayer

Because corporate prayer may take various forms—prayers of the people, pastoral prayer, collect—when Christians pray together, their collective imagination is formed and shaped in special ways.

Of all the times the word "saints" appears in the New Testament, it is never rendered in the singular.[8] The saints are always a

---

7. Haensch, "When Choirs Sing."

8. Wells, *Improvisation*, 43.

collective, a community. When we lift our hearts together, we are reminded that we are not alone. When we lift our hearts in prayer, we are reminded that we join all the saints. This brings both comfort and responsibility. Through corporate prayer, the holy Christian is reminded to rest in the Lord. They are reminded that there are those interceding on their behalf when they don't know what to pray. Not unrelated, the holy Christian is also reminded that they're responsible for their sister and brother. When other Christians can't pray for themselves, we must intercede.

The corporate prayers of the church are a holy habit that shapes us to live in community with other believers.

Preaching of the Scriptures

We live in a noisy world. From smartphones to twenty-four-hour news cycles, our eyes and ears are constantly being filled. If, as the saying goes, you are what you eat, you are also what you hear and see. The ways in which we view the world and the things we value are shaped by what we see and hear. The easy target here is young adults being shaped by the celebrity culture of social media. Celebrities have loud voices! But we must also recognize (confess?) that the voices of Fox News, CNN, Rush Limbaugh, and Trevor Noah are shaping how we perceive reality. Most of our churches have, at most, three hours of directed discipleship every week, while these competing voices captivate us for two to three hours *every day!* Then consider how sad it is when the pastor's sermon lasts longer than thirty minutes!

The preached word, then, serves as a pearl in the midst of the muck. The preaching reminds us that these other voices are not the only voices. By listening to the preached word, holy Christians are reminded of the one voice that should speak louder than any other. Through the preached word, holy Christians practice listening to the voice of the Lord above other competing voices. Preaching forms us to have singular fidelity to Christ and Christ's kingdom.

The Lord's Table

Arguably the most formational habit of holy Christians is the Lord's Supper, the Eucharistic meal. In his sermon "The Duty of Constant Communion," John Wesley writes,

> It is no wonder that men who have no fear of God should never think of doing this. But it is strange that it should be neglected by any that do fear God, and desire to save their souls; And yet nothing is more common. One reason why many neglect it is, they are so much afraid of "eating and drinking unworthily," that they never think how much greater the danger is when they do not eat or drink it at all. That I may do what I can to bring these well-meaning men to a more just way of thinking, I shall . . . show that it is the duty of every Christian to receive the Lord's Supper as often as he can.[9]

The duty of every Christian is to go to the Table as often as possible because in this act, we are explicitly receiving the life and practices of Christ within us. The Table of the Lord is completely a practice for holy living.

The holy habits formed in Communion are varied. First, we never *take* Communion; we always *receive* the body and blood of Christ. Since the grace of God is freely given and never based on merit, so is our participation in Communion based on the free grace of Christ. As such, our holiness is never taken—as if we merited that holiness. Holiness, like the free grace of Christ's atoning love, is always received.

Second, the broken bread and poured cup remind us that we are complicit in the death of Christ. The holy Christian is always aware of her sin, and she states with Paul, "The saying is sure and worthy of full acceptance, that Christ Jesus came into the world to save sin-

---

9. John Wesley, "Sermon 101: The Duty of Constant Communion," The Wesley Center Online, http://wesley.nnu.edu/john-wesley/the-sermons-of-john -wesley-1872-edition/sermon-101-the-duty-of-constant-communion/.

ners—of whom I am the foremost" (1 Tim. 1:15, NRSV). The sanctified believer is keenly aware of her need for Christ.

Third, the fermentation of the bread and the cup reminds us of the transformation that takes place in our lives because of Christ. The bread that was once a lump of flour, water, oil, and salt has, through fermentation, become a most fundamental source of life! While Nazarenes don't consume alcoholic wine during communion, the juice represents for us the fermented grape, also a source of life. When the Christian partakes of the fermented bread and cup, we're reminded of the patient ferment of the Spirit.[10] As God is always drawing us in, the sanctified one is always growing in the likeness of Christ. By eating fermented bread and drinking fermented drink (or something that symbolizes it), we practice our own spiritual fermentation: becoming like Christ.

Fourth, Christians from all walks of life come to the same Table. Christians with different upbringings, Christians of different socio-economic statuses, Christians of different races, Christians who speak different languages, Christians who voted for different political candidates, and Christians from different family systems all come to the same Table! The Eucharistic meal reminds the church that we are called to unity, and when we eat and drink of the same loaf and the same cup, we are reminded that these things that bind us together are stronger than the things that seek to divide us. Communion is a practice for sanctified believers to pursue unity with one another.

Finally, and most importantly, the consumption of the bread and cup is a reminder of the crucifixion of Christ. We are reminded as much when we read 1 Corinthians 11:26: "For whenever you eat this bread and drink this cup, you proclaim the Lord's death until he comes." The symbols of Christ's broken body and shed blood are consumed. If you are what you eat, then the Table is, for the holy Chris-

---

10. This popular phrase comes from Alan Kreider's text, *The Patient Ferment of the Early Church: The Improbable Rise of Christianity in the Roman Empire* (Grand Rapids: Baker Academic, 2016).

tian, a practice of giving ourselves away as Christ gave himself away. Communion forms within us the practice of *kenosis,* of self-emptying.[11] Christ's holiness was displayed most clearly by his willingness to give himself away completely for us. If sanctification isn't sacrificial, it isn't anything. Communion calls the Christian to commit herself to the *kenotic,* self-emptying love exemplified by Christ.

Benediction

If the Christian's first response to the world is to be called out, the second response to the world is to be called back in. To live a holy life is not to simply be separated from the world, but it is also to give one's life up to and for the world! If Christ came not to condemn the world but to save it (see John 3:16–17), his holy ones must follow suit. Richard Neuhaus writes, "To be converted away from the world toward this God is immediately to be converted back to the world. In other words, if we are truly converted to God in Christ, then we participate in his conversion to the world. We cannot love him if we do not share in his love for his creation."[12]

The benediction serves not to *dismiss* us, as if our work is complete when we walk out of the church doors. Quite the opposite, in fact! The benediction serves as a *sending* word. We're not dismissed, we're sent. The benediction scatters us to our various families, places of work, schools, communities, and neighborhoods on mission. As the holy ones of God, Christians don't exempt ourselves from caring for neighbor or community: that is our primary task! The church in the wilderness will need to keep holy practices in front of her. All that we do during worship is practiced so that we can go and love in the holy manner of Christ.

There are particular dangers holy people should avoid while worshiping in the wilderness. As we find life less certain than for-

---

11. See Philippians 2:1–11.

12. Richard John Neuhaus, *Freedom for Ministry* (Grand Rapids: William B. Eerdmans Publishing Company, 1992).

mer times, there are significant temptations. In Exodus 32 we read that while Moses was receiving the laws of YHWH, the people were getting restless. It's easy to get restless in the wilderness. They were wondering where God was. The things they once knew were no longer, and the presence of God felt far away. It's easy to feel that God's presence is far away in the wilderness. In the absence of Moses, what was Aaron to do?

We don't tell this part of Aaron's story favorably, but I'm thinking he constructed the golden calf with the best of intentions. If we go back twenty chapters, to Exodus 12, we see that when Israel fled Egypt, they didn't leave empty-handed; they plundered the Egyptians. Thus, while they were wandering in the wilderness, they had constant gold reminders of Egypt on their hands and hanging from their necks. Perhaps when Aaron collected their gold, it was so they could leave Egypt behind them. Perhaps Aaron was afraid he might "lose people," so in order to make people happy or keep the peace, he tried to curate a worship experience: the calf, then, may not have been intended to *replace* YHWH but to point the people of God *to* YHWH. Idolatry is rarely so blatant. In fact, when the calf was constructed, Aaron declared, "Tomorrow there will be a festival to the LORD" (Exodus 32:5).[13]

As sojourners in the wilderness, we will be tempted to curate worship experiences or to manufacture revival. These sincere attempts at crafting certainty during uncertain times will only distract from true sanctification. Holiness in the wilderness will look like radical fidelity to Christ. Holy folks believe that God is able to do all that needs to be done without our help. We will need to be reminded of this as we traverse these wild times.

---

13. Most English translations say LORD, but the Hebrew records the name of the Lord, YHWH.

7
WHY DIALOGUE WITH THE PAST?
A Russian Understanding of Holiness
OLGA DRUZHININA

ᕫᕬ

For many years, holiness language was part of Russian culture and mentality due to Russia's rich Christian heritage. The ideas related to holiness were developed and promoted in this part of Christendom for centuries. Many generations of monks and laypeople devoted their time to studying such aspects of holiness as a genuine spirit of love, humility, and an irrevocable self-denial. You may hear stories of "holy people" who played a special role in the history of this land. Even the country is often called "holy Rus," both in common conversations and in official speeches, which implies a special mission assigned to its people and land by God. Although most of the time people think of holiness as something unachievable for a common person in this earthly life, Orthodox Christians have their own understanding of who and what might be called holy. In addition, they treat "holy" people as well as "holy" objects with respect and honor. Therefore, the notion of holiness is important for them.

Being both Nazarene and Russian, I often ask myself the following questions: Can we learn something about holiness from this notable cultural heritage? Are there any special aspects of the holiness message that can be rediscovered in this context? This chapter is a result of reflection about the cultural factors and theological ideas related to holiness, which may inform and enrich our praxis.

Theological Background

Regardless of whether or not they know it, people in Russia have been dramatically influenced by the Orthodox Church. For centuries, Eastern Christianity has been shaping their thought patterns. Even if people never attended church, they were under its influence through Russian literature, philosophy, and national traditions because Russian religious culture "has left its mark on every cultural domain in the nation."[1] Therefore, it would be useful to discuss some ideas from the mainstream of Eastern theological thought.[2]

To begin, it is necessary to mention that one of the central doctrines of the Orthodox faith, which is closely connected to sanctification or holiness, is deification, or theosis. For Orthodox believers, this means to become like Christ, or "Christification."[3] This explains the Eastern idea of salvation, which is not "to satisfy a legal requirement, but to vanquish death."[4] Orthodox Christians believe

---

1. Jerry G. Pankhurst, "Religious Culture," in *Russian Culture at the Crossroads: Paradoxes of Postcommunist Consciousness*, ed. Dmitri N. Shalin (Boulder, CO: Westview Press, 1996), 128.

2. We will not discuss the views of Protestant churches in Russia because their influence was limited due to Russian law. Before 1917 it was "a violation of law for a person baptized into the Orthodox faith to convert to Protestantism." See Mark Elliott and Anita Deyneka, "Protestant Missionaries in the Former Soviet Union," in *Proselytism and Orthodoxy in Russia: The New War for Souls*, ed. John Witte, Michael Bourdeaux (Eugene, OR: Wipf & Stock, 2009), 197.

3. Panayiotis Nellas, *Deification in Christ: Orthodox Perspectives on the Nature of the Human Person* (Crestwood, NY: St. Vladimir's Seminary Press, 1987), 39.

4. Veli-Matti Karkkainen, *One with God: Salvation as Deification and Justification* (Collegeville, MN: Liturgical Press, 2004), 22.

that God alone is able to vanquish death because God is the immortal one. Christ as God incarnate saves people from death and helps them to become like him. Salvation, then, gives all people and the rest of creation the opportunity to be regenerated, to become immortal and incorruptible. On these terms, salvation in Eastern Christianity is not primarily viewed as liberation from sin, even though that is important, but "rather as return to life immortal and reshaping of the human being into the image of her creator."[5] Probably the closest idea to deification in the East is the imitation of Christ in the West. Still, theosis is something distinctly Eastern and more transcendent. However, the process of salvation is, in some sense, a process of attaining Christlike character and features, which implies becoming holy, as God is holy. The incarnation of our God makes it possible to sanctify humanity because Christ assumed the same human flesh.

Furthermore, it is very important to mention that the Orthodox understanding is always Trinitarian. According to Orthodox theology, humans can reestablish their likeness to Christ only through the grace of the Holy Spirit. Without the sanctifying work of the Spirit, it is impossible to reach the ultimate goal of holiness—participation in the triune God. The same Spirit enables people to keep fellowship with the Father and the Son in order to follow God's will in obedience and consecration. Orthodox believers have a deep sense of the necessity of grace. However, they believe that they have to cooperate with God and work together toward their holiness. As Vladimir Lossky writes, "For it is not a question of merits but of a cooperation, of a synergy of the two wills, divine and human, a harmony in which grace bears ever more and more fruit, and is appropriated—'acquired'—by the human person."[6] They view salvation in therapeutic terms as healing from sickness or injury, which implies the state of corruption after the fall. Orthodox believers and espe-

---

5. Karkkainen, *One with God*, 23.

6. Vladimir Lossky, *The Mystical Theology of the Eastern Church* (London: James Clarke & Co. Ltd., 1957), 198.

cially monks talk a lot about good deeds, but they have a different theological background. Their main goal is not to earn salvation or to please God but to become "healed," to become closer to God, and to become like God through the work of the Holy Spirit in their lives and through real transformation.

In Eastern thought, both Christology and Pneumatology are linked with the doctrine of deification, which teaches that the whole creation, material as well as spiritual, is to be redeemed and glorified. The incarnation of Christ is significant because it expresses a new attitude toward the human body and toward matter in general. The Eastern Fathers never asked "What is evil?" because the answer would imply that evil is something. They never connected evil with material things or with anything of substance. They believe that evil originates, therefore, in "the spiritual sin of the angel. And the attitude of Lucifer reveals to us the root of every sin: pride as revolt against God."[7]

Another perspective from which the Eastern Fathers discussed evil was that "evil is a lack, a vice, an imperfection: not a nature, but what a nature lacks to be perfect."[8] As John of Damascus puts it, "For evil is nothing else than absence of goodness, just as darkness also is absence of light."[9] In this sense, the real content of Orthodox faith is the "new creation" in Christ, when the whole creation will be transformed into its perfect state. This implies salvation of the body through material transfiguration and resurrection.[10] As Kallistos Ware writes, "Human beings are not saved *from* but *with* the ma-

---

7. Lossky, *Orthodox Theology: An Introduction* (Crestwood, NY: St. Vladimir's Seminary Press, 1989), 81. See also John of Damascus, "An Exact Exposition of the Orthodox Faith," 80; and Gregory Nazianzen, "On the Theophany, or Birthday of Christ," 347. Both in *Nicene and Post-Nicene Fathers* (Grand Rapids: William B. Eerdmans Publishing Company, 1971).

8. Lossky, *Orthodox Theology*, 80.

9. John of Damascus, "An Exact Exposition of the Orthodox Faith," 20.

10. This is the reason the Orthodox Church believes that the bodies of the holy people are partly transformed into a glorified state of being and therefore do not show signs of decay.

terial world; through humankind the material world is itself to be redeemed and transfigured."[11] In addition, they believe in "the Spirit-bearing potentialities of all material things."[12] The implication of this statement is the idea that holy objects (such as icons, a body of a saint, or land) can somehow contain the Holy Spirit, which was present in a saint during his or her earthly life. This also means that icons as well as the relics of the saints are able to transmit this Spirit to believers. In this sense, they are considered holy because they "become a vehicle of divine power."[13]

The Orthodox Church comes to a very positive conclusion about the potential of human beings to become sanctified and transformed during this present life. They believe that Mary, the mother of Jesus, was the first person who reached the complete state of deification. This means that her icons and the icons of the saints prove the fact that it is possible for humans to become deified/holy, or at least to go through some steps of transformation and deification in this life.[14] In the figure of Christ on the icons, we see the theological idea of "divinity made human," and through the icons of glorified saints, we can understand the other half of the Orthodox teaching—"humanity made divine."[15]

According to the Orthodox faith, all human beings have the potential to become saints without distinction of age, gender, or level of education. There are many examples of children who were canonized

---

11. Kallistos Ware, "The Spirituality of the Icon," in *The Study of Spirituality*, ed. Cheslyn Jones, Geoffrey Wainwright, and Edward Yarnold (Oxford: Oxford University Press, 1986), 197.

12. Ware, "The Spirituality of the Icon," 196.

13. Kenneth Parry, *Depicting the Word: Byzantine Iconophile Thought of the Eighth and Ninth Centuries* (Leiden, The Netherlands: E. J. Brill, 1996), 24.

14. See Leonid Ouspensky, "Icon and Art," in *Christian Spirituality: Origins to the Twelfth Century*, ed. Bernard McGinn, John Meyendorff, and Jean Leclercq (New York: SCM Press, 1989), 382.

15. See Jaroslav Pelikan, *Imago Dei: The Byzantine Apologia for Icons* (Princeton, NJ: Princeton University Press, 1990), 153.

by the church due to their exceptional behavior and lifestyle.[16] Icons of women and men are equally venerated in local churches across the country. People do not care about the social status of their saints during the saint's lifetime. It is not important whether the saint was from a noble family and well educated or a peasant and illiterate. People are looking for love, compassion, and wisdom of God that can be experienced and gained through communication with this saint, who can be alive or already in heaven. In this sense, they are looking for God, who may change their lives and fill them with meaning through the sanctifying Spirit.

Another important aspect of Eastern theology is its great emphasis on the social dimension of holiness. In the Orthodox Church, people are taught that they must have a spiritual guide, "a *pneumatikos pater* with whom the deepest thoughts of the soul will be shared."[17] We can find very often in the Eastern Church the appreciation of common life, or the life inside community. The doctrine of the unity of the church is very popular among Orthodox theologians. There is a special term for this kind of unity—*sobornost*, or conciliatoriness—the free association of people who have Christ as their head. Nicolas Berdyaev, a famous Russian philosopher, explains this as "the unity of love and freedom which has no external guarantees whatever."[18] This implies that Christians are supposed to help each other grow spiritually and teach each other. They also have to listen to those who have reached a higher level of spirituality. Kenneth Leech thinks that "the unity of the mystical and the social is something we have largely lost in the West. . . . The Orthodox know no such distinction. Both personal life of the heart and the cor-

---

16. The famous ones are children from the family of Tsar Nicolas II.

17. Kenneth Leech, "Introduction" in Tito Colliander's *Way of the Ascetics: The Ancient Tradition of Discipline and Inner Growth* (London: Mowbray, 1983), x.

18. Nicolas Berdyaev, *The Russian Idea* (New York: The Macmillan Company, 1948), 52.

porate life of the human society are to be transmigrated."[19] People have to strive for holiness not as isolated individuals but together, supporting their fellow believers, sharing each other's burdens as a community, experiencing God's grace as his children.

Common Perception of Holiness among People and the Ideas of Holiness in Russian Literature

It would be beneficial to see how this great theological heritage is processed and applied in everyday life by a common person in Russia. What are the qualities and characteristics that people treasure and consider holy? Whom do they adore as saints, and why? In Russian society, there has always been a conflict between people who consider themselves Christians and the hierarchical church. In the sixteenth through eighteenth centuries, the popular common form of holiness in Russia was "holy fools" or "folly in Christ."[20] They were rebels who did not want to obey the rules of the official church. As Andrzej de Lazari explains:

> They would wander about almost completely naked, with beams of wood on their shoulders, in chains, boldly reproaching the Tsars for the misdeeds of their reigns, they wept over the future fates of the nation and the motherland. Although the world would at times sneer at them, they unceasingly stigmatized the world's faults, praying for cities and people. Characteristic for them was their unwavering love for Christ and the Cross, freedom bordering on an anarchic individualism, disapproval of the "soft" life.[21]

Later in the nineteenth century, there was another movement of *starets,* or spiritual guides, inside the monasteries. In the consciousness of the Russian people, a *starets* was "a personification of 'unschooled' traditional Russian wisdom and a divine messenger."[22]

---

19. Leech, "Introduction," *Way of the Ascetics,* xi.

20. In Russian they are called *yurodivye* (юродивые).

21. Andrzej de Lazari, *The Russian Mentality: Lexicon* (Katowice, Poland: Slask, 1995), 127.

22. de Lazari, 104.

Most of the time, they were monks who provided spiritual directions to common people who came to visit a *starets* to share their suffering, to receive consolation, and to stay on "holy ground" for a while.[23] We can find the expression of this idea in Russian literature, such as in the classical novels of Fyodor Dostoevsky.

Russian classical literature, which provides many examples, may help us to understand how ideas of holiness are perceived by common people in Russia. As Boris Paramonov notes, leading national writers were able to "express the holistic consciousness . . . of elite and commoners alike."[24] The most authentic portraitists of the Russian soul are Fyodor Dostoevsky and Lev (Leo) Tolstoy. They are well known in the West and are referred to as guides to the Russian character, especially in relation to Christian ideas and ideals. Although they wrote more than a century ago, they are considered classics, and their perceptions of Russian mentality are commonly accepted as still relevant. For many Russian authors and for Dostoevsky in particular, the highest moral ideal was Christ. Therefore, the positive heroes more or less successfully imitate Christ's character and reflect virtues, which are considered by readers as signs of holiness or Christlikeness.

Both Dostoevsky and Tolstoy visited Optina Hermitage, the most celebrated center of "holy men" and its famous *starets*, Ambrose, who served as one of the prototypes for Father Zosima from Dostoevsky's final novel, *The Brothers Karamazov*. Through the lips of this character, Dostoevsky provides a great insight of Russian consciousness and shares with his readers what common Russian people would think of holiness and God. From this Father Zosima we can learn that "active love" leads to the knowledge of God and to the salvation of a person. When one of the heroines shares her doubts and asks for things that may convince her of God's existence, the answer is that she may know by the experience of active love:

---

23. There were some exceptions. For example, Grigori Rasputin was called *starets* at the court of Tsar Nicolas II.

24. Boris M. Paramonov, "Historical Culture," in *Russian Culture at the Crossroads*, 30.

"Strive to love your neighbor, actively and constantly. In so far as you advance in love you will grow surer of the reality of God and of the immortality of your soul. If you attain perfect self-forgetfulness in the love of your neighbor, then you will believe without doubt. Doubt will no longer be able to enter your soul. This has been tried. This is certain."[25]

This idea of love as a sign of close relationship with God is repeated throughout the whole novel. When another great saintlike character of this novel, Alyosha, recalls one of his last conversations with Zosima, the same theme of love runs through the whole admonition of a dying father. He starts with the words, "Love God's people." He persuades monks that they are not "holier than those that are outside" but says they are "responsible for all men and everything on earth."[26] He continues and explains what a person who strives for holiness should do:

For monks are not a special sort of men, but only what all men ought to be. Only through that knowledge, our heart grows soft with infinite, universal, inexhaustible love. Then every one of you will have the power to win over the whole world by love and to wash away the sins of the world with your tears. . . . Be not proud. Be not proud neither to the little nor to the great. . . . Love God's people. . . . Expound the Gospel to the people unceasingly. . . . Be not mercenary. . . . Do not love gold and silver, do not hoard them. . . . Have faith. Cling to the banner and raise it on high.[27]

Often in Russian literature and in the minds of people, this kind of love is related to suffering and humility. Patience, humility, and suffering are the greatest in the Russian system of values. It is especially true for suffering because "the theme of redemption through suffering is absolutely fundamental to Russian culture and central to

---

25. Fyodor M. Dostoevsky, *The Brothers Karamazov* (New York: Signet, 1986), 64. First published 1879–1880 in *The Russian Messenger*.

26. Dostoevsky, *Brothers*, 164.

27. Dostoevsky, *Brothers*, 164.

Compassion, or
co-suffering, is
important for a
Christian's
sanctification because
acts of charity done
to sufferers are
bearing witness
to Christ.

a great many views of Russian distinctiveness."[28] However, nobody is supposed to experience suffering for its own sake. The essence of "holy" suffering is self-sacrificial love or compassion. Even etymologically in the Russian language, the words "suffering" and "compassion" are related (*stradanie* and *so-stradanie,* respectively), where compassion means readiness to "suffer together" with another and share his or her life, literally following the words of the evangelist from the Gospel of John (15:13): "Greater love has no one than this: to lay down one's life for one's friends."

Compassion, or co-suffering, is important for a Christian's sanctification because acts of charity done to sufferers are bearing witness to Christ, to his death on the cross, and to his resurrection. One of the best examples from Dostoevsky is the willingness of his heroine from *Crime and Punishment,* Sonia, to share the sufferings of Raskolnikov, who murders two women and suffers from the guilt: "We are going to suffer together, we will bear the cross together!"[29] In this sense, Christlike co-suffering means showing love to those who are rejected by society: the afflicted, the wretched, the poor, and the sick. Interestingly enough, Sonia, who plays the role of a savior, is far from being a saint because she is a prostitute. However, a reader has the feeling that both of these characters are moving toward holiness. In some sense, there is an impression that they are "resurrected" by Christ when Sonia, the prostitute, reads to Raskolnikov, the murderer, the biblical story of the raising of Lazarus.[30] Love and co-suffering make them closer to God and open a way for salvation, for transformation into "new creatures," into Christlikeness.

The theme of holy suffering was so popular in Russia that there was a specific national form of a cult of saints who suffered— *strastoterptsy.* They are adored for their constant readiness in all cir-

28. Tim McDaniel, *The Agony of the Russian Idea* (Princeton, NJ: Princeton University Press, 1996), 34.

29. Dostoevsky, *Crime and Punishment* (Oxford: Oxford University Press, 2008), 405. First published 1866 in *The Russian Messenger.*

30. Dostoevsky, *Crime and Punishment,* 342.

cumstances to suffer and to give their lives for their motherland and the nation. However, they were canonized "not for their patriotism but because it was for them a way to fulfill the commandment of Christ to love."[31] They were humble, obedient, and full of forgiveness. Most of them gave away their money, and many ended their lives in a monastery after rejecting the world in the name of God and their neighbors. This self-sacrificial love and readiness to suffer for the good of the people elevated them to sainthood in the eyes of other Christians.

As we already noted, humility is another important saintly characteristic that is admired by common people. They believe that this virtue is an essential aspect of holiness.[32] It often goes together with meekness of heart, patience, and submissiveness. The opposing concept would be rebellion and pride. Therefore, humility is believed to be one of the means of doing battle with evil powers.[33] In this sense, God's grace will save and protect a humble person from anything harmful in this life. However, the way of salvation may include his or her death, which this person is supposed to accept without complaint.

The best example of such behavior can be found in Tolstoy's novel *War and Peace*, in which his character Platon Karataev opposes violence through nonresistance. Platon keeps telling stories illustrating God's inexplicable goodness and mercy. Mostly he shares his wisdom that God oversees everything and that happiness can be found in the appreciation of a simple life. He is a simple, illiterate peasant, but he is an honest person of integrity. He is not a saint in the full sense of this word, but Tolstoy attributes to him the qualities that would lead to a holy life.[34] Karataev represents simplicity, kindness, peacefulness, and, above all, humility and love. He is able to love everything and

---

31. de Lazari, *Russian Mentality*, 108.

32. See this idea in Pierre Pascal's *The Religion of the Russian People* (Crestwood, NY: St. Vladimir's Seminary Press, 1976), 32.

33. de Lazari, *Russian Mentality*, 99.

34. Tolstoy deliberately put himself outside of the official Orthodox Church. He used the language of Christianity, but he did not believe in anything supernatural, including the divinity of Christ.

everyone, including French soldiers who hold him captive. Through this character, Tolstoy is trying to illustrate a love, universal and unchanging, like God's love for his whole creation.

This kind of love is often revealed in the life stories of the Russian saints. For example, it is believed that St. Sergius of Radonezh shared his bread with a bear while living in a forest as a young monk. This leads us to another virtue that is related to humility and highly prized in the eyes of the people: *zhalost,* or pity, though the English word does not capture the full meaning.[35] It is a deep feeling of compassion for all created things—humans, birds, and animals—whereby people cannot bear to see any creature suffering. When this *zhalost* is felt for humans, it leads to a practical realization of holiness—to generous hospitality, sharing sorrows, and satisfying the needs of anyone who is around.

In Russian culture, humility often implies respect for others and the refusal to pass judgment. In addition to this, Christian holiness is grounded in forgiveness, charity, peace, and brotherhood. Individuals cannot be considered holy if they do not serve society in one way or another. In the mentality of the people, a saint is a link between God and the rest of the people. If we ask the question "Who is a saint?" an answer could be found in a commonly repeated phrase: "God reveals himself in a mysterious way through his saints" ("Дивен Бог во святых своих").[36] Holy people are the ones through whom God can be seen and glorified.

Therefore, the saints are people who strive for purity and holiness while at the same time their lives serve as a revelation of God, his love, and his mighty power, which may create miracles. But also, and most importantly, it is essential to note that this revelation is supposed to happen through a participation in communal life. Humility, co-suffering, sacrificial love, and pity describe the Russian

---

35. See also Pierre Pascal, *The Religion of the Russian People* (Crestwood, NY: St. Vladimir's Seminary Press, 1976), 31.

36. There is another common phrase, similar in meaning to the first one: "God is glorified through his saints" ("Славен Бог во святых Своих").

spirit of community experienced as *sobornost,* or conciliatoriness. The church assures the believers that God works in his saints and through their actions and attitude toward others. On these terms, people believe that saints continue to intercede for them even after their death, and then serve as guardians. Saints are seen as co-sufferers with the needy and neglected. However, they are able to share joyful moments with other believers as well. Therefore, people believe in the invisible presence of their saints during the liturgy and church services. In this sense, the holy people are honored as the living witnesses of God's faithfulness and his unlimited grace.

Finally, we can add that the standards of holiness in Russian society are related to selfless dedication to God and to neighbor, which implies uncritical love and compassion. Many people devoted themselves to ministry in hospitals, orphanages, or monasteries in order to implement what they believed God called them to do for those less fortunate. Some of them were considered holy or saints not because they were blameless or without mistake but because of their sacrificial love, which testified to the presence of God in their lives. The next generation of Christians is in great debt to those who saved and developed this evangelical attitude, which helps to share the gospel even without words.

Conclusion

This overview of the different aspects of Orthodox theology and the religious thought patterns of people in Russia makes it apparent that the attitude toward holiness in this context is complex. Although Orthodox believers seem to us to be quite different in their practice and worship, they may contribute to our understanding of holiness. We should not dismiss the richness of this great heritage. There are many things we have in common as followers of Christ. For example, an interpretation of sanctification as gaining Christlikeness corresponds to our own understanding. We also believe that the saints exemplify transformation, which is done by the indwelling grace of the Holy Spirit. There is a common basic theology that bears witness to the reality of God, but there are many nuances that can be learned if we spend time listening and watching their lives and practices.

We do not talk very much about suffering or co-suffering. Therefore, this adds a different shade of meaning to our understanding of holiness. Some theologians believe that this is a spiritual finding that can be offered to the world because "their suffering has become a profound treasury of hard-won experience that has quietly elicited spiritual growth and reflectiveness. . . . That stamps the human spirit with a special beauty."[37] As Christians, we know that we live in the age of *not yet*, which implies that we can certainly experience physical weakness, suffering, temptation, and death. In this regard, it is beneficial for us to learn from others how to keep our faith and hope while genuinely anticipating the consummation of this world and transfiguration into the new creation.

The theological emphasis on the social aspect of holiness may open for us a wider perspective. The present experience of corporate worship, when previous generations of faithful believers are remembered and graciously thanked, may teach us to respect the great achievements of Christians who lived and served before us. The slightly different approach to the question of soteriology, when salvation is understood as renewal and restoration of humanity as a whole, proves helpful. This makes us reformulate a less corporate but more individualistic and forensic approach to the doctrine of salvation and holiness as its part. We have to remember that God's plan is not only to redeem individuals but also to form a community—to recreate a new humanity—that will be characterized by love, compassion, humility, pity, and selflessness.

The Trinitarian understanding of God and his work of transformation in human life may serve as a starting point for our explanation of holiness. This can lead us to new discoveries related to the problem of mistakes in the lives of holy people. This complex issue,

---

37. Thomas C. Oden, *Two Worlds: Notes on the Death of Modernity in America and Russia* (Downers Grove, IL: InterVarsity Press, 1992), 153–54.

As a community
of believers, we are
called to proclaim
a biblically sound
doctrine of
Christian holiness.

which remains a problem among theologians, can be addressed from a personal and relational perspective when God's love, not our own effort, is the biggest factor that plays its role in our sanctification. The idea of synergy—cooperation with God and progressive perfection under the guidance of a more experienced instructor—sounds promising. This practice can be rediscovered and applied in our communities of faith that are discipleship-oriented.

However, the Orthodox interactions with their tradition and holy objects may raise some questions that require more detailed research and analysis. Although the idea of Christian holiness is an authentic part of Eastern theology, some beliefs need to be questioned in the light of Scripture. In a sense, we have to guard our holiness message against inappropriate interpretations and false assumptions. We can provide theologically coherent answers and a fresh way of thinking that is in dialogue with the past but not limited by ancient tradition.

As a community of believers, we are called to proclaim a biblically sound doctrine of Christian holiness, but it should be presented in culturally relevant terms. We have to find ways to model God's holiness before people in the local context. It would be wonderful if our commitment to holiness and compassion could be demonstrated in deed as well as in word. Then compassion may pave the way to salvation and allow believers to manifest their holiness as co-suffering and love. We could not agree more with Dostoevsky: "If you love, you are of God. . . . All things are atoned for, all things are saved by love."[38]

We can learn one more thing from this culture: sanctification, perfection, or holiness is not our goal in itself. The real purpose of our existence is the glorification of God through our lives when the mighty acts of our Creator are revealed to the whole world. With this in mind, we have to share our holiness message to move closer to God and to become people through whom his love and grace might be spread to others.

---

38. Dostoevsky, *Brothers*, 60.

WHY HOLINESS?
A Beautiful and Mighty Chorus
CARLA SUNBERG
ॐ

We have taken a journey as we have explored why we should embrace the unique doctrine of holiness. Often in the Old Testament, holiness was compared to beauty. From one of the early church fathers we read, "For Beauty has in its own nature an attractiveness for everyone who looks at it. So, if the soul becomes clean of all evil, it will exist entirely in beauty. The divine is beautiful by its own nature. The soul will be joined to the divine through purity."[1] In this state of beauty we can become partakers of the divine nature, and together, the whole church can become a beautiful and mighty chorus of holiness.

To be a faithful follower of Jesus Christ means much more than just "getting by." It also means we are fully engaged in our relationship with him and are continually being transformed into his likeness. In his second epistle, Peter encourages us to think about holiness and the divine nature in this way:

> Thus he has given us, through these things, his precious and very great promises, so that through them you may escape from the corruption that is in the world because of lust, and may be-

---

1. Gregory Nyssen, *DAR* (PG 46:89D).

come participants of the divine nature. For this very reason, you must make every effort to support your faith with goodness, and goodness with knowledge, and knowledge with self-control, and self-control with endurance, and endurance with godliness, and godliness with mutual affection, and mutual affection with love. For if these things are yours and are increasing among you, they keep you from being ineffective and unfruitful in the knowledge of our Lord Jesus Christ.
(2 Pet. 1:4–8, NRSV)

This section of Scripture is an invitation into the holy life, which is the calling for each and every single follower of Jesus Christ. God's desire for all God's children is that we become "participants of the divine nature." This is laid out clearly for us in verse 4, and then the following verses take us into an account of how we grow, ever reaching to higher heights of our faith.

Albert Barnes says, "We should add one virtue to another, that we may reach the highest possible elevation in holiness."[2] Each virtue becomes a voice in what will become a mighty and beautiful chorus of holiness in our own lives. Too often we have thought that, once we have experienced entire sanctification, we have finished the journey—but in many ways, becoming entirely sanctified is only the beginning. Just as in marriage, once the wedding ceremony is over, we are completely and totally married, but we also know that the relationship between two married people will continue to grow and flourish throughout a lifetime spent together. Therefore, as we live the sanctified life, we must have an ever-increasing participation in God that is accomplished through the practice of virtues.

Just imagine that it all begins with the single voice of faith, as pointed out in verse 5 of the 2 Peter scripture. The voice sings out that it believes in God and trusts in God, but it is a single voice. Next, that faith must become lived out in acts of goodness. Suddenly

---

2. Albert Barnes, *Notes, Explanatory and Practical, on the General Epistles of James, Peter, John, and Jude* (London: Knight and Son, 1854), 276.

Becoming
entirely sanctified
is
only the
beginning.

the solo voice becomes a beautiful duet, and the two voices play off each other as they bring a balance to the spiritual life—but this is still not enough. The duet continues as we grow in grace and take time to become students of God, whether through intimacy in a relationship, through prayer and worship, or through the study of the incarnate *logos* of God revealed through the written Word. All this study leads to knowledge, and suddenly there is a beautiful trio of sound. Peter's addition of knowledge to this harmonious display is important because of the infiltration of Gnosticism in his day. There were those who believed that knowledge alone could separate them from the physical world they deemed evil. No, Peter says: knowledge without faith and goodness is nothing, and the foundation must always be faith.

The chorus of holiness continues to build as we add to our lives the voice of self-control. Self-control becomes the bass voice that provides a protective lower barrier to the activities of life that can drag us down and out of our relationship with God. And that is why the next voice must be added, the one of endurance, for unless self-control has endurance it will not sustain us when temptation occurs. We are in this for the long haul. We need to be breathing the very air of God for the song to be beautiful and to endure throughout our lifetime.

Now, add to that chorus the voice of godliness. Somehow, I imagine this to be a beautiful soprano voice that sings out clear above the rest in a way that energizes the entire chorus, sparking the song onward, into a beautiful tapestry of rich glory. The song becomes more and more glorious—like when we hear the "Hallelujah Chorus" and somehow believe we have experienced heaven on earth! There is something transcendent about that song—and so the chorus of our lives transcends the things of this earth as we participate in the divine nature. This is holiness. When the world experiences our holy song, they too are drawn to the Author of our faith.

But this is not the end, for though we have heard the mighty chorus, there are two more voices that must be added. Tucked in the midst of it all is the voice of mutual affection. It may not be the most beautiful voice in the entire chorus—it may actually be the inclusion of a voice that is weaker than the rest—but the chorus is strengthened by its inclusion. It is a voice that reaches out to and loves deeply other brothers and sisters who are growing in their faith. No matter how strong or weak their voices, no matter how on or off key, they are drawn into the mighty chorus of holiness, for the chorus is now so strong that they will blend in and have the joy of experiencing that transcendent love of God.

The final voice added to the mighty chorus—for, as we learn to have mutual affection for one another, we become consumed with the overarching divine nature—is love. And suddenly the whole chorus is drawn into a holy hush as, in unison, we sing the "amen" of God's pure nature: holy love.

Through the practice of virtue, "we become an image of the image, having achieved the beauty of the Prototype through activity as a kind of imitation, as did Paul, who became an 'imitator of Christ,' through his life of virtue."[3] One of our early church fathers, Gregory of Nyssa, said that "by coming closer to the inaccessible Beauty you have yourself become beautiful, and like a mirror, as it were, you have taken on my appearance"—meaning the beautiful appearance of the bridegroom.[4] "Hence the Word says to her: You have become fair because you have come near to my light, and by this closeness to me you have attracted this participation in beauty."[5] In this transformation, attention is no longer paid to outward beauty; attention is paid to the beauty found within as we reflect Christ and participate in him.

Why holiness? Because a world filled with God's children reflecting the image of Jesus and singing the beautiful music of the holy life becomes a vision of the already present kingdom of God.

Soli Deo Gloria

---

3. Nyssen, *DP* (GNO III.I) (FC, 111). Nyssen quotes 1 Cor. 4:16.
4. Nyssen, *CC*, Homily 4 (PG 44:832-833c) (GNO VI), trans. Musurillo, 171.
5. Ibid.